The Complete Medicare Handbook

U.S. Department of Health and Human Services

Edited and expanded by **Eugene Landay**
Program Director of Health Insurance
Counseling and Advocacy Program

Prima Publishing & Communications
P.O. Box 1260MED
Rocklin, CA 95677
(916) 624-5718

Production by Carol Dondrea, Bookman Productions
Typography by Compositors Corporation
Interior design by Renee Deprey
Cover design by The Dunlavey Studio

Prima Publishing & Communications
Rocklin, CA

Library of Congress Cataloging-in-Publication Data

The complete medicare handbook / the U.S. Department of Health and Human Services.
p. cm.
ISBN 1-55958-036-4
1. Medicare—Handbooks, manuals, etc. I. United States. Dept. of Health and Human Services.
HD7102.U4C5817 1990
344.73'0226—dc20
[347.304226] 90-32814
CIP

90 91 92 93 RRD 10 9 8 7 6 5 4 3 2 1
Printed in the United States of America

How to Order:

Quantity discounts are available from the publisher, Prima Publishing & Communications, P.O. Box 1260MED, Rocklin, CA 95677; telephone (916) 624-5718. On your letterhead include information concerning the intended use of the books and the number of books you wish to purchase.

U.S. Bookstores and Libraries: Please submit all orders to St. Martin's Press, 175 Fifth Avenue, New York, NY 10010; telephone (212) 674-5151.

Contents

Repeal of the Medicare Catastrophic Coverage Act

I. General Information on Repeal and Transition Back to Prior Law

1. Repeal of the Medicare catastrophic benefit provisions of the Medicare Catastrophic Coverage Act (MCCA) means that Medicare benefits available as of January 1, 1990, are the same as those under prior law. Thus:

   - The Medicare program will pay for the first 60 days of inpatient hospital care per "spell of illness" after the beneficiary pays one hospital deductible ($592 in 1990). A "spell of illness" begins on admission to a hospital or skilled nursing facility, and ends 60 days after discharge.

- If a beneficiary is hospitalized for more than 60 days, coinsurance is required for days 61–90 ($148 per day in 1990).
- All beneficiaries are entitled to 60 "lifetime reserve days" of care, which they may use at any time; coinsurance of $296 per day is required for lifetime reserve days.
- Beneficiaries are entitled to 100 days of care in a skilled nursing facility only after an individual has been transferred to the facility from a hospital in which he or she was a patient for not less than three consecutive days before being discharged in connection with the transfer. Medicare pays for the first 20 days of care; coinsurance is required on days 21–100 ($74 per day in 1990).
- A beneficiary is entitled to 210 days of hospice care (two periods of 90 days and one subsequent period of 30 days).

2. The supplemental premium (commonly known as the "surtax") has been *repealed retroactively.* It is as if it were never enacted. *Beneficiaries will not be liable for the surtax when they file their 1990 tax returns* (due April 1991).

   A decision regarding an IRS informational mailing to all Medicare beneficiaries is pending. The IRS has no plans for either a press release or notification.

3. The *Medicaid provisions* of MCCA *were not repealed.* Thus the Medicaid buy-in for beneficiaries at or below the poverty line was retained, protection from "spousal impoverishment" was retained, and Medi-

caid coverage for certain pregnant women and infants was retained.

4. The *flat premium* increase under Part B is repealed, effective January 1, 1990. It was expected to take the Social Security Administration about three months to reprogram its computers to reflect the changes in the law; the change should have been corrected by April or May 1990 Social Security checks. The excess flat premium dollars collected will be refunded later in the year.
5. The *"maintenance of effort"* provisions of MCCA, which required certain employers to provide additional benefits or refunds to beneficiaries equal to the value of the benefits in their plans which duplicated Medicare's new catastrophic coverage, is repealed, effective January 1, 1990.
6. Most minor, technical, health-related corrections to the 1987 Omnibus Budget Reconciliation Act were retained.

II. Protection for Covered Beneficiaries

Hospital Benefits

No day before January 1, 1990, is counted for purposes of determining the beginning of a spell of illness. Thus beneficiaries in a hospital on December 31, 1989, and discharged after January 1, 1990, are deemed to have begun a new spell of illness on January 1. However:

- No additional deductible will be imposed on a beneficiary who paid a deductible for hospitalization in December 1989 if the beneficiary has a spell of illness that began in January 1990.
- No deductible will be imposed on an individual for care in a spell of illness which began before January 1990.
- Lifetime reserve days used *before*, but not in, 1989 are counted. Thus, for example, if an individual used 10 lifetime reserve days in 1987 and 15 in 1988, only 35 lifetime reserve days are available after January 1, 1990.

Skilled Nursing Facility Benefits

An individual may receive—subject to the three-day prior-hospitalization rule—100 days of Medicare-covered care in a skilled nursing facility (SNF) per spell of illness. Coinsurance is required from days 21–100. However, the three-day prior-hospitalization rule is waived for individuals who were in an SNF on December 31, 1989, and who are discharged after January 1, 1990. The three-day prior-hospitalization rule remains waived until the beneficiary is out of an SNF or hospital for 30 consecutive days.

Hospice Benefits

The repeal of the extended hospice benefit does not apply to any beneficiary who elected hospice benefit extension prior to January 1, 1990.

III. Revision of Supplemental Medicare Health Insurance ("Medigap") Policies

1. The National Association of Insurance Commissioners (NAIC) has 90 days after the date of enactment to revise its model "Medigap" regulation to reflect repeal of the MCCA. The amended regulation would then become the standard that a private policy would have to meet to be certified by the federal government as a Medicare supplemental policy. If the NAIC does not so act within 90 days, the Secretary of Health and Human Services is required to issue federal model standards within 60 days.
2. States are given one year to adopt legislative or regulatory changes that would produce a certification requirement at least as stringent as that required by the revised NAIC model.
3. Insurers are required to have sent to policyholders, by January 31, 1990, a notice explaining the changes in benefits by repeal and how these changes affect premiums and benefits.
4. If a policyholder had Medigap coverage as of December 31, 1988, but dropped that coverage, insurers would be required to give the policyholder, for at least 60 days beginning not later than February 1, 1990, the option of reinstating previous coverage, as of January 1, 1990, under the following conditions: (a) no waiting period for pre-existing conditions; (b) "substantially equivalent" coverage in effect before termination; (c) premiums "at least as favorable to the policyholder" had coverage not been terminated.

1

Using Your Medicare Handbook

This chapter tells you about:

Your Medicare handbook is designed to help you determine whether the services you need are covered by Medicare and how program payments are made. It is intended to be a handy reference to help you understand how the Medicare program works and to know what your benefits are. There is an alphabetical index at the back to assist you in finding information on specific subjects. Though Medicare pays for many of your health care expenses, *it does not cover all of them.* Therefore, it is important for you to know in advance what Medicare does and does not pay for.

Handbook Highlights

- Page 71 provides a list of the services and supplies that Medicare cannot pay for.
- Chapter 4 (pages 53–61) tells you how to submit your medical insurance claims.
- Beginning on page 145 is an address list showing you where to send your medical insurance claims.
- Chapter 5 (pages 63–67) tells you what to do if you disagree with a Medicare decision or the amount of payment on a claim.

If you have questions not answered by this handbook or would like additional information, you may call your Medicare carrier. Telephone numbers are listed on pages 145–159 of this handbook. Or you may call your Social Security office.

People eligible for Medicare because of kidney disease should consult Supplement I, "Medicare Coverage of Kidney Dialysis and Kidney Transplant Services" on page 93.

What Is Medicare?

The Medicare program is a federal health insurance program for people 65 or older and certain disabled people. It is run by the Health Care Financing Administration of the U.S. Department of Health and Human Services. Social Security Administration offices across the country take applications for Medicare and provide general information about the program.

The Two Parts of Medicare

There are two parts to the Medicare program. **Hospital insurance** (Part A) helps pay for inpatient hospital care, some inpatient care in a skilled nursing facility, home health care, and hospice care. **Medical insurance** (Part B) helps pay for medically necessary doctors' services, outpatient hospital services, home health care, and a number of other medical services and supplies that are not covered by the hospital insurance part of Medicare.

Both parts of Medicare have amounts that you must pay out-of-pocket (premiums, deductibles, coinsurance payments) or through coverage by another insurance plan. These out-of-pocket amounts are set each year, according to formulas established by Congress. New payment amounts begin each January 1. When amounts increase, you will be notified.

Intermediaries and Carriers

The federal government contracts with private insurance organizations called *intermediaries* and *carriers* to make Medicare payments. *Intermediaries* make coverage and payment decisions on services in hospitals, skilled nursing facilities, home health agencies, and hospices. *Carriers* handle claims for services by doctors and other suppliers covered under Medicare's medical insurance program.

Peer Review Organizations

Peer review organizations (PROs) are groups of practicing doctors and other health care professionals who are paid by the federal government to review the hospital care of Medicare patients. Each state has a PRO to help Medicare decide whether care is reasonable and necessary, is provided in the appropriate setting, and meets the standards of quality accepted by the medical profession. PROs have the authority to deny payments if care is not medically necessary or not delivered in the most appropriate setting. In addition, PROs respond to requests for review of hospital notices of noncoverage issued to beneficiaries, and PROs respond to hospital requests for reconsideration of PRO decisions. PROs also investigate individual patient complaints. If you are admitted to a Medicare-participating hospital, you will receive "An Important Message from Medicare," which explains your right as a hospital patient and provides the name, address, and phone number of the PRO for your state. A copy of the message is printed on pages 81–87.

If you feel that you are improperly refused admission to a hospital or that you are forced to leave the hospital too soon, ask for a written explanation of the decision. Medicare regulations require that such a written notice must fully explain how you can appeal the decision, and it must give you the name, address, and phone number of the peer review organization where your appeal or your request for review can be submitted. (See Chapter 5 for a more complete discussion of your appeal rights under Medicare.)

Providers of Services and Suppliers

Providers of services and certain suppliers under Medicare must meet all licensing requirements of state or local health authorities. They must also meet additional Medicare requirements before payments can be made for their services. Medicare providers must also comply with Title VI of the Civil Rights Act, which prohibits discrimination because of race, color, or national origin. Your Social Security office can tell you whether the provider is Medicare-certified.

Medicare cannot pay for care you receive from a hospital, skilled nursing facility, home health agency, hospice, or outpatient rehabilitation provider that is not certified to participate in the program. Such providers are referred to as nonparticipating. Certain suppliers of services, too, must be Medicare-approved for Medicare to pay for their services. Medicare cannot pay for care you receive from the following suppliers unless they are certified: ambulatory surgical centers, independent physical therapists, independent occupational therapists, clinical laboratories, portable X-ray suppliers, dialysis facilities, and rural health clinics.

In some cases, Medicare *can* help pay for emergency care in a qualified nonparticipating hospital. If you need assistance, any Social Security office can help you file the claim.

The Private Health Plan Option

In addition to the traditional fee-for-service Medicare option, Medicare offers the private health plan option.

Under this arrangement, many prepayment plans such as health maintenance organizations (HMOs) and competitive medical plans (CMPs) have contracts with Medicare. These plans receive direct payments from Medicare for services covered by both hospital insurance (Part A) and medical insurance (Part B).

HMOs and CMPs generally cover most of your health care costs, with fixed monthly premiums and minimal copayments. Many of them offer additional services beyond what Medicare covers at no additional cost—such things as preventive care, dental care, hearing aids, and eyeglasses. HMOs and CMPs also reduce the amount of paperwork you have because you generally do not have to file any claims.

If you are thinking about choosing an HMO or CMP, there are some requirements and restrictions that you must consider:

1. You must be enrolled in Medicare's medical insurance (Part B) and continue to pay your Part B premium.
2. You must live within the geographic area that is served by the HMO or CMP under Medicare contract.
3. If you have chosen hospice care, you are ineligible to enroll in an HMO or CMP as long as the hospice choice remains in effect. However, after you become a member of an HMO or CMP, you may elect to receive hospice benefits; you will not be required to disenroll from the HMO or CMP.
4. If you have end-stage renal disease, you are not allowed to enroll in an HMO or CMP. However, if you are a member of an HMO or CMP and develop end-stage renal disease, you cannot be disenrolled.

5. You will usually be required to receive all care from the HMO or CMP, except in emergency situations.

If you already belong to a Medicare HMO or CMP, there are some options you should know about. First, you may disenroll from the HMO/CMP at any time. Disenrollment can be handled by your plan or your local Social Security office. Second, if you feel that you have received poor-quality care, you have several choices for action: (1) You have access to the prepayment plan's grievance procedures. (2) You may complain to your peer review organization (PRO) or quality review organization (QRO). (3) If you feel further appeal is appropriate, you can exercise your appeal rights—rights that are similar to those you are guaranteed under traditional fee-for-service Medicare (see page 66).

If you want to know whether there are prepayment plans with Medicare contracts in your area, contact a Social Security office. If you wish to obtain information about how to enroll in an HMO or CMP, what benefits are provided, and what the membership rules are, you should contact the HMO or CMP directly.

For more information, see Supplement IV, "Medicare and Prepayment Plans," on page 123.

Your Medicare Card

The Medicare card (see page 14) shows the Medicare coverage you have (hospital insurance, medical insurance, or both) and the date your protection started. If you don't have both parts of Medicare, see Chapter 7 for information on how you may obtain the part you don't have.

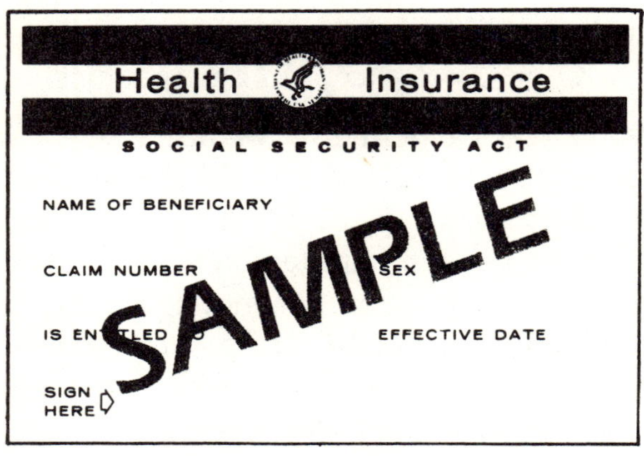

Your card also shows your health insurance claim number. Sometimes this claim number is referred to as your Medicare number. The claim number has nine digits and a letter. On some cards, there may also be another number after the letter. Your full claim number must always be included on all Medicare claims and correspondence. When a husband and wife both have Medicare, each will receive a separate card and claim number. Each spouse must use the exact name and claim number shown on his or her card.

It is important that you remember to:

1. Always show your Medicare card when you receive services that Medicare can help pay for.
2. Always write your health insurance claim number (including the letter) on any bills you send in and on any correspondence about Medicare. Also, you should have your Medicare card available when you make a telephone inquiry.
3. Carry your card with you whenever you are away

from home. If you ever lose it, immediately ask your Social Security office to get you a new one.

4. Use your Medicare card only after the effective date shown on it.
5. Never permit someone else to use your Medicare card.

Buying Health Insurance to Supplement Medicare

Medicare provides basic protection against the high cost of health care, but it will not pay all of your medical expenses, nor most long-term care expenses. For this reason, many private insurance companies sell insurance to supplement Medicare. The federal government does not sell or service such insurance.

If you are thinking about buying private insurance to supplement your Medicare protection, you should shop carefully. Supplement V, "Guide to Health Insurance for People with Medicare," on page 129 explains how supplemental insurance works and how to shop for it. It also lists the names, addresses, and telephone numbers of state insurance departments and state agencies on aging. These offices can provide you valuable help in making your decision about whether to buy insurance to supplement Medicare.

There are federal criminal and civil penalties (fines) for certain actions in selling health insurance to supplement Medicare. These penalties may be imposed against any insurance agent or company that knowingly sells you a policy that duplicates Medicare coverage or any private health insurance that you already own, but that will not pay duplicate benefits. Penalties also apply if insurance agents misrepresent to you that they are employees or agents of the Medicare program or of any government agency. There is also a penalty for making a false statement about a policy's meeting legal standards for certification when it does not, and for using the mails in a state for delivering advertisements of health insurance policies to supplement Medicare if the policies have not been approved for sale in that state.

If you suspect that you have been the victim of these or any other illegal sales practices, you should contact your state insurance department. The telephone numbers to call are listed on pages 161–172. Also, you may call this federal Medicare toll-free number: 1-800-888-1998.

Fraud and Abuse Hotline

If you have reason to believe that a doctor, hospital, or other health care provider is performing unnecessary or inappropriate services or is billing Medicare for services you did not receive, you may call a toll-free hotline installed by the Department of Health and Human Services' Inspector General to receive any evidence of such fraud or abuse of the Medicare program: 1-800-368-5779. In Maryland, call 1-800-638-3986. **Please do not call the Inspector General's hotline for Medicare policy questions or questions about delayed claims or payments.**

2

Hospital Insurance

This chapter tells you about:

The Prospective Payment System

Medicare pays for most inpatient hospital care under the **prospective payment system (PPS)**. Under PPS, hospitals are paid fixed amounts based on the principal diagnosis for each Medicare hospital stay. In some cases, the Medicare payment will be more than the hospital's costs; in other cases, the payment will be less than the hospital's costs. In special cases, where costs for necessary care are unusually high, or the length of stay is unusually long, the hospital receives additional payment.

It is important to remember that this system does not change your Medicare hospital insurance protection as described in this handbook. It does not determine the length of your stay in the hospital or the extent of care you receive. The law requires participating hospitals to accept Medicare payments as payment in full, and those hospitals are prohibited from billing the Medicare patient for anything other than the applicable deductible amounts, plus any amounts due for non-covered items or services, such as television, private duty nurses, or cosmetic surgery.

Kinds of Care Covered

Medicare hospital insurance helps pay for four kinds of care: (1) inpatient hospital care; (2) medically necessary inpatient care in a skilled nursing facility; (3) home health care; and (4) hospice care.

PART A (1990): HOSPITAL INSURANCE, BENEFIT PERIOD

Length of stay	Beneficiary Pays	Medicare Pays
First 60 days	First $592	Balance
61st to 90th days	$148 per day	Balance
91st to 150th days	$296 per day	Balance
Beyond 150 days	All	None
Skilled Nursing		100% first 20 days
	$74 per day, 21st through 100th day	Balance
Hospice Care	5% or a maximum of $592 per year	210 days
Home Health Care		21 days

After the deductible of $592 in 1990, Medicare pays most expenses for the next 60 days in a benefit period.

Skilled nursing facility care is the only type of nursing home care that Medicare covers. *Medicare does not pay for care that is primarily custodial.* Medicare hospital insurance will pay for most but not all of the services you receive in a hospital or skilled nursing facility or from a home health agency or hospice program. There are covered services and noncovered services under each kind of care. Covered services are services and supplies that hospital insurance can pay for.

You do not have to send Medicare any bills for care you receive from a participating hospital, skilled nursing facility, home health agency, or hospice. Medicare will pay your benefits directly to the place where you received the care.

Whenever a hospital, skilled nursing facility, home health agency, or hospice sends Medicare a hospital insurance claim for payment, you will get a Medicare Benefit Notice that explains the decision made on the claim. If you have any questions about the notice, get in touch with the office shown on the notice.

When You Are a Hospital Inpatient

Medicare hospital insurance can help pay for inpatient hospital care if all of the following four conditions are met:

1. A doctor prescribes inpatient hospital care for treatment of your illness or injury.
2. You require the kind of care that can be provided only in a hospital.
3. The hospital is participating in Medicare.

4. The utilization review committee of the hospital or a peer review organization does not disapprove your stay.

If you meet these four conditions, Medicare will pay for medically necessary inpatient hospital care according to the following "spell of illness" schedule:

- For the 1st through the 60th day of confinement, you pay a deductible of $592; Medicare will pay the balance.
- For the 61st through the 90th day, you pay $148 per day; Medicare will pay the balance of medically necessary care.
- For confinement from the 91st through the 150th day, you pay $296 per day; Medicare pays the balance.
- Days 1 through 60 will be reinstated after you have been out of the hospital for a period of 60 consecutive days.
- Days 91 through 150 can never be reinstated.
- If you paid a hospital deductible for your first confinement, you do not have to pay another deductible, if you are not out of the hospital for 60 days, when you return for any additional care.

Major services covered when you are a hospital inpatient

Medicare hospital insurance can pay for these services:

- a semiprivate room (two to four beds in a room)

- all your meals, including special diets
- regular nursing services
- cost of special care units, such as intensive care unit, coronary care unit, etc.
- drugs furnished by the hospital during your stay
- blood transfusions furnished by the hospital during your stay (see below for information about coverage of blood)
- lab tests included in your hospital bill
- X-rays and other radiology services, including radiation therapy, billed by the hospital
- medical supplies such as casts, surgical dressings, and splints
- use of appliances, such as a wheelchair
- operating and recovery room costs, including hospital costs for anesthesia services
- rehabilitation services, such as physical therapy, occupational therapy, and speech pathology services

Some services not covered when you are a hospital inpatient

Medicare hospital insurance cannot pay for these services:

- personal convenience items that you request such as a telephone or television in your room
- private duty nurses
- any extra charges for a private room unless it is determined to be medically necessary

....

Note: If you disagree with a decision on the amount Medicare will pay on a claim or whether services you receive are covered by Medicare, you always have the right to appeal the decision (see Chapter 5).

Coverage of Blood Under Hospital Insurance

Hospital insurance can help pay for blood (whole blood or units of packed red blood cells), blood components, and the cost of blood processing and administration. If you receive blood as an inpatient of a hospital or skilled nursing facility, hospital insurance can pay all of these blood costs, except for any nonreplacement fees charged for the first three pints of whole blood or units of packed red cells per calendar year. The nonreplacement fee is the charge that some hospitals and skilled nursing facilities make for blood that is not replaced.

You are responsible for the nonreplacement fees for the first three pints or units of blood furnished by a hospital or skilled nursing facility. If you are charged nonreplacement fees, you have the option of either paying the fees or having the blood replaced. If you choose to have the blood replaced, you can either replace the blood personally or arrange to have another person or a blood assurance plan replace it for you. A hospital or skilled nursing facility cannot charge you for any of the first three pints of blood you replace or arrange to replace. (See page 46 for explanation of coverage of blood under Medicare medical insurance.)

Care in a Psychiatric Hospital

Hospital insurance can help pay for no more than 190 days of care in a participating psychiatric hospital in your lifetime. Once you have used these 190 days, hospital insurance cannot pay for any more care in a psychiatric hospital.

Also, there is a special rule that applies if you are in a participating psychiatric hospital at the time your hospital insurance starts. Any Social Security office can give you information about this special rule.

Care in a Foreign Hospital

Medicare generally cannot pay for hospital or medical services outside the United States. (Puerto Rico, the U.S. Virgin Islands, Guam, American Samoa, and the Northern Mariana Islands are considered part of the United States, along with the 50 states and the District of Columbia.) However, it can help pay for care in qualified Canadian or Mexican hospitals in three situations. These are: (1) You are in the United States when an emergency occurs and a Canadian or Mexican hospital is closer than the nearest U.S. hospital that can provide the emergency services you need. (2) You live in the United States, and a Canadian or Mexican hospital is closer to your home than the nearest U.S. hospital that can provide the care you need, regardless of whether an emergency exists. (3) You are in Canada traveling by the most direct route to or from Alaska and another state and an emergency occurs that requires that you be admitted to a Canadian hospital.

When hospital insurance covers your inpatient stay

in a Canadian or Mexican hospital, your medical insurance can cover necessary doctors' services and any required use of an ambulance. If the hospital does not submit the claim to Medicare, any Social Security office will help you get Medicare payment for the covered services you receive. If you are planning to travel overseas, you may want to inquire about the availability of special short-term health insurance for foreign travel.

Care in a Christian Science Sanatorium

Medicare hospital insurance can help pay for inpatient hospital and skilled nursing facility services you receive in a participating Christian Science sanatorium if it is operated or listed and certified by the First Church of Christ, Scientist, in Boston.

Skilled Nursing Facility Care

Medicare hospital insurance can help pay for inpatient care in a Medicare-certified skilled nursing facility if your condition requires daily skilled nursing or rehabilitation services that, as a practical matter, can be provided only in a skilled nursing facility.

A **skilled nursing facility** is a specially qualified facility that has the staff and equipment to provide skilled nursing care or rehabilitation services and other related health services. Most nursing homes in the United States are not skilled nursing facilities, and many skilled nursing facilities are not certified by Medicare. In some facilities, only certain portions are certified to participate in Medicare. If you are not sure whether a facility or a particular portion is certified to participate in Medicare as a skilled nursing facility, ask someone at the facility or call a Social Security office.

Hospital insurance can help pay for care in a skilled nursing facility if the following conditions are met:

1. An individual has been transferred to the facility from a hospital in which he or she was a patient for not less than three consecutive days prior to the transfer.
2. A doctor certifies that you need, and you actually receive, skilled nursing or skilled rehabilitation services on a daily basis.
3. The Medicare intermediary or the facility's utilization review committee does not disapprove your stay.

Both conditions must be met. But it's especially important to remember the requirement that you must need skilled nursing care or skilled rehabilitation services on a daily basis.

Skilled nursing care means care that can only be performed by, or under the supervision of, licensed nursing personnel. Skilled rehabilitation services may include such services as physical therapy performed by, or under the supervision of, a professional therapist. The skilled nursing care and skilled rehabilitation services you receive must be based on a doctor's orders.

Hospital insurance cannot pay for your stay if you need skilled nursing or rehabilitation services only occasionally, such as once or twice a week, or if you do not need to be in a skilled nursing facility to get skilled services. Also, hospital insurance cannot pay for your stay if you are in a skilled nursing facility mainly because you need custodial care (see Chapter 6).

When your stay in a skilled nursing facility is covered by Medicare, hospital insurance can help pay for up to 100 days a calendar year, but only if you need daily skilled nursing care or rehabilitation services for that long.

If you are admitted to a skilled nursing facility, Medicare will pay all costs for the first 20 days. If you are still confined as a skilled nursing patient after 20 days, you will pay $74 per day up to the 100th day. Medicare will pay the difference, but only up to the 100th day. Medicare does not provide any coverage after you have been a skilled nursing patient for 100 days.

Hospital insurance does not cover your doctor's services while you are in a skilled nursing facility. Medicare medical insurance covers doctors' services. Chapter 3 tells you how medical insurance helps with doctor bills.

Major services covered when you are in a skilled nursing facility

Medicare hospital insurance can pay for these services:

- a semiprivate room (two to four beds in a room)
- all your meals, including special diets
- regular nursing services

- rehabilitation services, such as physical, occupational, and speech therapy
- drugs furnished by the facility during your stay
- blood transfusions furnished to you during your stay (see page 22 for information about coverage of blood)
- medical supplies such as splints and casts
- use of appliances such as a wheelchair

Some services not covered when you are in a skilled nursing facility

Medicare hospital insurance cannot pay for these services:

- personal convenience items that you request such as a television in your room
- private duty nurses
- any extra charges for a private room unless it is determined to be medically necessary
- custodial nursing home care services provided to persons with chronic, long-term illnesses or disabilities

---

Note: If you disagree with a decision on the amount Medicare will pay on a claim or whether services you receive are covered by Medicare, you always have the right to appeal the decision (see Chapter 5).

Home Health Care

If you need part-time skilled health care in your home for the treatment of an illness or injury, Medicare can pay for covered home health visits furnished by a participating home health agency. A **home health agency** is a public or private agency that specializes in giving skilled nursing services and other therapeutic services, such as physical therapy, in your home. (A facility that mainly provides skilled nursing or rehabilitation services cannot be considered your home.)

Medicare can pay for home health visits only if all of the following four conditions are met:

1. The care you need includes intermittent skilled nursing care, physical therapy, or speech therapy.
2. You are confined to your home.
3. A doctor determines you need home health care and sets up a home health plan for you.
4. The home health agency providing services is participating in Medicare.

Once these conditions are met, either hospital insurance or medical insurance can pay for all medically necessary home health visits. When you no longer need intermittent skilled nursing care, physical therapy, or speech therapy, Medicare can continue to pay for home health visits if you need occupational therapy.

Medicare does not cover general household services, meal preparation, shopping, or other home care services furnished mainly to assist people in meeting personal, family, or domestic needs.

Home health services covered

Medicare can pay for these services:

- part-time or intermittent skilled nursing care
- physical therapy
- speech therapy

If you need intermittent skilled nursing care, physical therapy, or speech therapy, Medicare can also pay for:

- occupational therapy
- part-time or intermittent services of home health aides
- medical social services
- medical supplies
- durable medical equipment (80% of approved cost)

Home health services not covered

Medicare cannot pay for these services:

- full-time nursing care at home
- drugs and biologicals
- meals delivered to your home
- homemaker services
- blood transfusions

Medicare pays the full approved cost of all covered home health visits. You may be charged only for any services or costs that Medicare does not cover.

The home health agency will submit the claim for payment. You don't have to send in any bills yourself.

Note: If you disagree with a decision on the amount Medicare will pay on a claim or whether services you receive are covered by Medicare, you always have the right to appeal the decision (see Chpater 5).

Hospice Care

A **hospice** is a public agency or private organization that is primarily engaged in providing pain relief, symptom management, and supportive services to terminally ill people and their families.

Medicare hospital insurance can help pay for hospice care if all of the following three conditions are met:

1. A doctor certifies that a patient is terminally ill.
2. A patient chooses to receive care from a hospice instead of standard Medicare benefits for the terminal illness.
3. Care is provided by a Medicare-certified hospice program.

Special benefit periods apply to hospice care. Hospital insurance can pay for two 90-day periods and one subsequent 30-day period. A beneficiary may disenroll from the hospice during either 90-day period and return to regular Medicare coverage, then later re-elect the hospice benefit.

There are no deductibles under the hospice benefit. Medicare pays the full cost of all covered services for the terminal illness, except for small coinsurance amounts for outpatient drugs and inpatient respite care. The patient is responsible for 5% of the cost of outpatient drugs or $5 toward each prescription, whichever is less. For inpatient respite care, the patient pays 5% of the Medicare-allowed rate (approximately $3.25 per day in 1989). The rate varies slightly depending on the geographic area of the country.

Respite care is a short-term inpatient stay, which may be necessary for the patient, to give temporary relief to the person who regularly assists with home care. Each inpatient respite care stay is limited to no more than five days in a row.

While receiving hospice care, if a patient requires treatment for a condition not related to the terminal illness, Medicare continues to help pay for all necessary covered services under the standard Medicare benefit program.

Hospice services covered

Medicare hospital insurance can pay for these services for beneficiaries as part of hospice care:

- nursing services
- doctors' services
- drugs, including outpatient drugs for pain relief and symptom management

- physical therapy, occupational therapy, and speech-language pathology
- home health aide and homemaking services
- medical social services
- medical supplies and appliances
- short-term inpatient care, including respite care
- counseling

....

The Medicare hospital insurance hospice benefit *cannot* pay for treatments other than for pain relief and symptom management of a terminal illness.

Note: If you disagree with a decision on the amount Medicare will pay on a claim or whether services you receive are covered by Medicare, you always have the right to appeal the decision (see Chapter 5). For more information on hospice benefits, turn to Supplement II, "Hospice Benefits Under Medicare," on page 113).

3

Medical Insurance

This chapter tells you about:

Medicare medical insurance can help pay for (1) doctors' services, (2) outpatient hospital care, (3) diagnostic tests, (4) durable medical equipment, (5) ambulance service, and (6) many other health services and supplies not covered by Medicare hospital insurance.

The following sections will tell you more about these different kinds of care, the services that are and are not covered by medical insurance, and what part of your medical expenses Medicare can pay.

PART B (1990): MEDICAL INSURANCE FOR A CALENDAR YEAR

Premium in 1990 is $28.60 per month

Services	Beneficiary Pays	Medicare Pays
	$75 deductible	None
Doctors (limited psychiatric service)	20% of approved amount	80% of *approved* amount after the deductible is paid
Hospital Outpatient Department	20% of approved amount	80% of *approved* amount after the deductible is paid
Other Ambulance Durable medical equipment Lab test Physical therapy (limited) Prosthetic devices X-ray and radiation Other	20% of approved amount	80% of *approved* amount after the deductible is paid

If the provider/supplier has not accepted the assignment method, the beneficiary will also be responsible for the amount beyond the approved amount.

Deductible and Coinsurance Amounts

Medicare requires that a beneficiary assume a percentage of the costs of covered services. This requirement is known as **coinsurance**. After you have paid $75 in approved charges (see above) for covered medical expenses in a calendar year, medical insurance generally will pay 80% of the approved charges for any additional covered services you receive during the rest of the year. You are responsible for the remaining 20%. Medicare will determine the "approved" or "reasonable" charge for each service you receive.

The first $75 in covered expenses is called the medical insurance **deductible**. You need to meet this $75 deductible only once during the year. The deductible can be met by any combination of covered expenses. You do not have to meet a separate deductible for each different kind of covered service you might receive.

The deductible applies to your expenses related to doctors, providers, and suppliers. Suppliers are persons or organizations other than doctors and health care facilities that furnish equipment or services covered by medical insurance.

Covered Doctors' Services

Medicare medical insurance can help pay for covered services you receive from your doctor in his or her office, in a hospital, in a skilled nursing facility, in your home, or any other location in the United States. Your medical insurance can also help pay for doctors' services you receive in connection with covered inpatient care in a Canadian or Mexican hospital. See page 23 to find out about care in Canadian and Mexican hospitals.

Major doctors' services covered

Medicare medical insurance can help pay for these services:

- medical and surgical services, including anesthesia
- diagnostic tests and procedures that are part of your treatment
- radiology and pathology services by doctors while you are a hospital inpatient or outpatient
- other services that are ordinarily furnished in the doctor's office and included in his or her bill, such as:
    - X-rays
    - services of your doctor's office nurse
    - drugs and biologicals that cannot be self-administered
    - transfusions of blood and blood components
    - medical supplies
    - physical/occupational therapy and speech pathology services

Some doctors' services not covered

Medicare medical insurance cannot pay for these services:

- most routine physical examinations and tests directly related to such examinations
- routine foot care
- eye or hearing examinations for prescribing or fitting eyeglasses or hearing aids
- immunizations (except pneumococcal vaccinations or immunizations required because of an injury or immediate risk of infection, and hepatitis B for certain persons at risk)

- cosmetic surgery unless it is needed because of an accidental injury or to improve the function of a malformed part of the body

Chiropractors' Services

Medical insurance helps pay for only one kind of treatment furnished by a licensed, Medicare-certified chiropractor. The only treatment that can be covered is manual manipulation of the spine to correct a subluxation that can be demonstrated by X-ray. Medical insurance does not pay for any other diagnostic or therapeutic services, including X-rays, furnished by a chiropractor.

Podiatrists' Services

Medical insurance can help pay for any covered services of a licensed podiatrist, including the removal of plantar warts. Treatment of mycotic toenails (a fungus infection) is limited to once every 60 days unless the medical necessity for more frequent treatment is documented by your physician or podiatrist.

Medical insurance generally does not cover routine foot care such as hygienic care; treatment for flat feet or other structural misalignments of the feet; and removal of corns, calluses, and most warts. But medical insurance can help pay for routine foot care if you have a medical condition affecting the lower limbs (such as severe diabetes) which requires that such care be performed by a podiatrist or a doctor of medicine or osteopathy.

Dental Care

Medical insurance can help pay for dental care only if it involves (1) surgery of the jaw or related structures, (2) setting fractures of the jaw or facial bones, or (3) services that would be covered when provided by a doctor. If you need to be hospitalized because of the severity of a dental procedure, Medicare can cover your hospital stay even if the dental care itself is not covered by Medicare.

Care in connection with the treatment, filling, removal, or replacement of teeth; root canal therapy; surgery for impacted teeth; and other surgical procedures involving the teeth or structures directly supporting the teeth generally are not covered.

Optometrists' Services

Medicare can help pay for the vision care services of optometrists, if the services are among those already covered by Medicare and if the optometrist is legally authorized to perform such services in your state. However, Medicare will not pay for routine eye exams, and it will not pay for eyeglasses or corrective lenses unless they are prosthetic lenses that replace the natural lens of the eye.

Second Opinion Before Surgery

Sometimes your doctor will recommend surgery for the treatment of a medical problem. In some cases, surgery is unavoidable. But there is increasing evidence that many conditions can be treated equally well without surgery. Because even minor surgery involves some risk, we recommend that you get a second doctor's opinion to help you decide about surgery. Medical insurance will help pay for a second opinion in the same way it pays for services by doctors.

Your own doctor is the best source for referral to another doctor. But if you wish, you can call the Health Care Financing Administration's Second Surgical Opinion Hotline for the names and phone numbers of doctors in your area who provide second opinions. The toll-free number is 1-800-638-6833 (in Maryland 1-800-492-6603).

Other Medical Services

Outpatient Hospital Services

Medicare medical insurance helps pay for covered services you receive as an outpatient from a participating hospital for diagnosis or treatment of an illness or injury. Under certain conditions, medical insurance can also help pay for emergency outpatient care you receive from a nonparticipating hospital.

When you go to an **outpatient facility** for outpatient services, be sure to show the people there your most recent "Explanation of Medicare Benefits" notice. From this form, they usually can tell how much of the $75 deductible you have met.

If the hospital cannot tell how much of the $75 deductible you have met and the charge for the services

ss than $75, the hospital may ask you
bill. The amount you pay the hospital
ward any part of the deductible you
any medical insurance payments due
will be paid directly to you.

Major outpatient hospital services covered

Medicare medical insurance helps pay for these services:

- services in an emergency room or outpatient clinic
- laboratory tests billed by the hospital
- X-rays and other radiology services billed by the hospital
- medical supplies such as splints and casts
- Drugs and biologicals that cannot be self-administered
- blood transfusions furnished to you as an outpatient

Some outpatient hospital services not covered

Medicare medical insurance cannot pay for these services:

- routine physical examinations and tests directly related to such examinations
- eye or ear examinations to prescribe or fit eyeglasses or hearing aids

- immunizations (except pneumococcal and hepatitis B vaccinations, or immunizations required because of an injury or immediate risk of infection)
- routine foot care

....

Hospital Outpatient Mental Health Services

Medicare can help pay for mental health care in a hospital outpatient program for treatment of mental illness, so long as a doctor certifies that your treatment is necessary and that without treatment you would require hospitalization.

After you have met the $75 yearly deductible, Medicare will pay 80% of the cost of this hospital outpatient care. This benefit is not subject to the hospital insurance lifetime limit of 190 days of inpatient hospitalization for treatment of mental illness. Nor is it subject (except in the case of physician services) to the medical insurance payment limit of $1,100 per year for outpatient treatment of mental illness at facilities other than hospitals (see page 47).

Ambulatory Surgical Services

Some surgery can be performed safely on an outpatient basis, avoiding the need for an inpatient hospital stay. Medicare can pay 80% of the center's approved fee for certain specified outpatient surgical procedures performed in a Medicare-certified ambulatory surgical center. The center can be affiliated with a hospital or it can be independent, but it must provide only ambulatory surgery services and must have an agreement with Medicare to do so.

After you have met the $75 deductible, Medicare will pay 80% of your surgeon's and anesthesiologist's approved charge for services. Such services can include pre- and postoperative care furnished on an outpatient basis in an ambulatory surgical center in a hospital.

Outpatient Physical and Occupational Therapy and Speech Pathology Services

Medicare medical insurance can help pay for medically necessary outpatient physical and occupational therapy or speech pathology services if all of the following three conditions are met:

1. Your doctor must prescribe the service.
2. Your doctor or therapist must set up a plan of treatment.
3. Your doctor must periodically review that plan.

You may receive physical therapy, occupational therapy, or speech pathology services as an outpatient of a participating hospital or skilled nursing facility, or from a home health agency, clinic, rehabilitation agency, or public health agency approved by Medicare. The organization providing services always submits the claim and may charge you only for any part of the $75 deductible you have not met, 20% of the remaining approved amount, and any noncovered services.

You may receive services directly from an independently practicing, Medicare-certified physical or occupational therapist in his or her office or in your home if such treatment is prescribed by a doctor. But the maximum amount that medical insurance can pay for these services is $400 a year. The medical insurance payment would be less than $400 if charges for these services are used to meet part or all of your $75 deductible. Either you or the therapist can submit the claim as described in Chapter 4.

Comprehensive Outpatient Rehabilitation Facility Services

Under certain circumstances, Medicare can help pay for outpatient services you receive from a comprehensive outpatient rehabilitation facility (CORF). Covered services include physicians' services; physical, speech, occupational, and respiratory therapies; counseling; and other related services. You must be referred by a physician who certifies that you need skilled rehabilitation services. For most CORF services, you are responsible only for the annual deductible and 20% of the Medicare-approved charges. For mental health treatment in a CORF, the maximum Medicare can pay is $1,100 a year for physicians' services and CORF services combined.

Independent Clinical Laboratory Services

Medical insurance can pay the full approved fee for covered clinical diagnostic tests provided by independent laboratories that are certified to perform them. The laboratory must accept assignment for these tests (see page 49). It may not bill you for the tests. If a doctor prescribes tests the laboratory is not certified to perform, Medicare cannot pay for the tests, and you can be required to pay for them. Not all laboratories are certified by Medicare, and some laboratories are certified only for certain kinds of tests. Your doctor can usually tell you which laboratories are certified and whether the tests he or she is prescribing from a certified laboratory are covered by medical insurance. Your doctor must accept assignment (agree to receive the insurance payment directly from Medicare) for covered clinical diagnostic laboratory tests that he or she furnishes. He or she may not bill you for them.

Portable Diagnostic X-ray Services

Medical insurance helps pay the approved charges for portable diagnostic X-ray services you receive in your home if they are ordered by a doctor and if they are provided by a Medicare-certified supplier.

Ambulance Transportation

Medical insurance can help pay for medically necessary ambulance transportation but only if (1) the ambulance, equipment, and personnel meet Medicare requirements, and (2) transportation in any other vehicle could endanger the patient's health.

Under these conditions, medical insurance can help pay for ambulance transportation to a hospital or skilled nursing facility, or from a hospital or skilled nursing facility to your home. Also, if you are an inpatient in a hospital or skilled nursing facility which cannot provide a medically necessary service you need, medical insurance can help pay for round trip ambulance transportation to the nearest appropriate facility.

Medical insurance cannot pay for ambulance use from your home to a doctor's office.

Medical insurance usually can help pay for ambulance transportation only in your local area. But if there are no local facilities equipped to provide the care you need, medical insurance will help pay for necessary ambulance transportation to the closest facility that can provide the necessary care. If you choose to go to another institution that is farther away, Medicare payment still will be based on the reasonable charge for transportation to the closest facility.

Necessary ambulance services in connection with a covered inpatient stay in a Canadian or Mexican hospital (see page 23) can also be covered by medical insurance.

Durable Medical Equipment

Medical insurance can help pay for durable medical equipment such as oxygen equipment, wheelchairs, and other medically necessary equipment that your doctor prescribes for use in your home. (A facility that mainly provides skilled nursing or rehabilitation services cannot be considered your home.)

On January 1, 1989, new rules went into effect that govern whether durable medical equipment must be rented or purchased. In general, durable medical equipment that costs more than $150 must be rented. Inexpensive durable medical equipment can be either purchased or rented. Your carrier will be able to provide more specific guidance on these rules.

Blood

Medical insurance can help pay for blood and blood components you receive as an outpatient or as part of other covered services, except for any nonreplacement fees charged for the first three pints or units received in each calendar year. After you have met the $75 deductible, medical insurance pays 80% of the approved charges for blood, starting with the fourth pint in a calendar year.

Prosthetic Devices

Medical insurance helps pay for prosthetic devices needed to substitute for an internal body organ. These include Medicare-approved corrective lenses needed after a cataract operation, colostomy or ileostomy bags and certain related supplies, and breast prostheses (including a surgical brassiere) after a mastectomy. Medical insurance can also help pay for artificial limbs and eyes, and for arm, leg, back, and neck braces. Orthopedic shoes are covered *only* when they are part of leg braces and the cost is included in the orthopedist's charge. Dental plates or other dental devices are not covered.

Pneumococcal Vaccine

Medical insurance will pay the full approved charges for pneumococcal vaccine and its administration. Neither the $75 annual deductible nor the 20% coinsurance applies to this service.

Hepatitis B Vaccine

Medicare will help pay for hepatitis B vaccine administered to beneficiaries considered to be at high or intermediate risk of contracting the disease.

Medical Supplies

Medical insurance can also help pay for surgical dressings, splints, casts, and similar medical supplies ordered by a doctor in connection with your medical treatment. This does not include adhesive tape, antiseptics, or other common first-aid supplies.

Other Covered Services and Supplies

Medical insurance helps pay for rural health clinic services; dialysis services; physician assistant, certified registered nurse anesthetist, nurse-midwife, and psychologist services; and for antigens and blood clotting factors. Some providers of these services are required to take assignment (accept the insurance payment directly from Medicare). The person or group who furnishes your service should be able to tell you whether you can file the Medicare claim or whether they must file the claim for you.

Outpatient Treatment of Mental Illness

Doctors' services and comprehensive outpatient rehabilitation facility services you receive for outpatient treatment of a mental illness are covered under a special payment rule, but the maximum amount medical insurance could pay in 1989 for these services was $1,100. The medical insurance payment would have been less than $1,100 if charges for these services were used to meet part or all of your $75 deductible. (Medicare coverage of hospital outpatient treatment of mental illness is described on page 41; Medicare coverage of treatment of mental illness in a comprehensive outpatient rehabilitation facility is described on page 43.)

Participating Doctors and Suppliers

Doctors and suppliers can sign agreements to become Medicare **participating doctors or suppliers**. This means they have agreed in advance to accept assignment on all Medicare claims. Doctors and suppliers are given the opportunity to sign participation agreements each year. Medicare-participating doctors and suppliers can display emblems or certificates that show they accept assignment on all Medicare claims.

The names and addresses of Medicare-participating doctors and suppliers are listed by geographic area in the *Medicare-Participating Physician/Supplier Directory.* You can get the directory for your area free of charge from your Medicare carrier (see page 145), or you can call your carrier and ask for names of some participating doctors in your area. Also, this directory is available for review in all Social Security offices, state and area offices of the Administration on Aging, and in most hospitals.

Assignment

The **assignment** method, in which the doctor or supplier receives the medical insurance payment directly from Medicare, can save you time and money. When the assignment method is used, the doctor or supplier agrees to accept the charge approved by the Medicare carrier for the covered services. Medicare pays your doctor or supplier 80% of the approved charge, after subtracting any part of the $75 deductible you have not met. The doctor or supplier can charge you only for the part of the $75 deductible you have not met and for the coinsurance, which is the remaining 20% of the approved charge. Of course, your doctor or supplier also can charge you for any services that Medicare does not cover.

	Actual Charge	Medicare-Approved Charge	Medicare Pays	You Are Responsible For
Doctor Accepts Assignment	$500	$400	$320 (80% of approved charge)	$80 (20% of approved charge)
*Doctor Does Not Accept Assignment	$500	$400	$320 (80% of approved charge)	$180 (difference between actual charge and Medicare payment)

* Medicare law requires doctors who do not take assignment for elective surgery to give you a written estimate of your out-of-pocket costs if the total charge is $500 or more.

If your doctor does not accept assignment, Medicare pays you 80% of the approved charge, after subtracting any part of the $75 deductible you haven't met. The doctor can bill you his or her actual charge. On page 49 are examples of the two payment methods (in both examples, the $75 deductible has already been met).

Participating Providers

Hospitals, skilled nursing facilities, home health agencies, comprehensive outpatient rehabilitation facilities, and providers of outpatient physical and occupational therapy and speech pathology services are all participating providers under Medicare medical insurance. They submit their claims directly to Medicare—you cannot submit claims for their services. The medical insurance payment made to the provider relieves you of responsibility for 80% of the provider's charges for the covered services you receive, after subtracting any part of the $75 deductible you have not met. The provider will charge you for the part of the deductible you have not met, plus 20% of the billed charges.

Medicare Benefits Notice

After you or the doctor or supplier sends in a medical insurance claim, Medicare will send you a notice called "Explanation of Medicare Benefits" to tell you the decision on the claim.

This notice shows what services were covered,

what charges were approved, how much was credited toward your $75 yearly deductible, and the amount Medicare paid. Please examine the notice carefully. If you believe payment was made for a service or supply you didn't receive, or the payment is otherwise questionable, you may call the carrier that handled your claim. The carrier's toll-free number appears on the notice, and a list of the numbers for all member carriers is given on pages 145 through 159 of this handbook. You must contact the carrier yourself.

Approved or "Reasonable" Charges

Medicare medical insurance payments are based for the most part on what the law defines as **reasonable charges**, or the amounts approved by the Medicare carrier. Because of the way the approved amounts are determined and because of high rates of inflation in medical care prices, the charges approved are often less than the **actual charges** billed by doctors and suppliers. Medical insurance usually pays only 80% of the approved charge even if it is less than the actual charge.

When a medical insurance claim that is reimbursable on a reasonable charge basis is submitted, the carrier compares the actual charge shown on the claim with the customary and prevailing charges for that service. The charge approved by the carrier will be: the **customary charge** (the charge most frequently made by the doctor or supplier for each item or service), the **prevailing charge** (based on all the customary charges in the locality for each type of service), or the actual charge—whichever is the lowest.

4

How to Submit Medical Insurance Claims

This chapter tells you about:

Submitting Your Medical Insurance Claim

If the doctor or supplier participates in Medicare, uses the assignment method of payment, or chooses to submit an unassigned claim for you, he or she submits the **claim**.

If the doctor or supplier does not accept assignment and does not submit the claim for you, you submit the claim, using the "Patient's Request for Medicare Payment" form, also called Form 1490S (see page 88 for a sample form 1490S). It must be submitted to the Medicare carrier for medical insurance to pay for covered services of doctors and suppliers. All Social Security offices and Medicare carriers, and most doctors' offices, have copies of the form. Instructions on how to fill it out are on the back of the form. Complete and sign the form; attach itemized bills for services you received.

An itemized bill must show (1) the date you received the services, (2) the place where you received the services, (3) a description of the services, (4) the charge for each service, (5) the doctor or supplier who provided the services, and (6) your name and your health insurance claim number, including the letter at the end of the number. If the bill doesn't include all of this information, your payment will be delayed. It is also helpful if the nature of your illness (diagnosis) is shown on the bill. If you are submitting a claim for the rental or purchase of durable medical equipment, you must include the bill from the supplier and the doctor's prescription. The prescription must show the equipment you need, the medical reason for the need, and an estimate of how long the equipment will be medically necessary.

You may submit several itemized bills with a 1490S form. It doesn't matter whether all the bills are from one doctor or supplier or from different people who gave you services. You can send in the bills either before or after you pay them.

Before any medical insurance payment can be made, your record must show that you have met the deductible. So as soon as your bills come to $75 in a calendar year, send them to your Medicare carrier with a 1490S form. Page 60 tells you where to send your claim. Once you have met the $75 deductible, we suggest that you send in your future bills for covered services as soon as you get them so that Medicare payments can be made promptly.

If all your medical bills for the year amount to less than $75, medical insurance cannot pay any part of your bills for the year.

It's a good idea to keep a record of your medical insurance claim in case you ever want to inquire about it. Before you send in a claim, write down the date you mail it, the services you received, the date and charge for each service, and the name of the person who provided each service.

If you need to get information from your Medicare carrier about your claim record or find out more about a particular claim, you must write or call the carrier personally.

There are special rules for submitting your medical insurance claim if you are a member of an HMO or CMP. If you are a member of an HMO or CMP and you receive a bill for medical services, equipment, or supplies, you may have to send the bill to your HMO or CMP for processing. You can find out who should process the claim by consulting your HMO/CMP membership handbook, or contacting your HMO/CMP.

When Other Insurance Pays First

If any of the following insurance situations applies to you, please notify your doctor, hospital, or other provider of services and, except in the case of liability claims, file your claim with the other insurer first. You may want to file liability claims with Medicare first.

When You or Your Spouse Continues to Work

Medicare has special rules that apply to beneficiaries who have employer group health plan coverage through their employment or the employment of a spouse.

Employers with 20 or more employees are required to offer workers and their spouses age 65 and over the same health insurance benefits offered to younger workers and spouses. In such situations you and your spouse have the option to accept or reject your employer's health plan. If you accept it, Medicare will become the secondary payer. If you reject your employer's health plan, Medicare will remain the primary health insurance payer. If you elect Medicare to be the primary payer, your employer cannot offer you coverage that supplements Medicare.

For more information, contact your employer or turn to Supplement III, "Medicare and Employer Health Plans," on page 119.

If You Are Disabled and Under Age 65

If certain disabled beneficiaries have coverage under an employer's health plan or the health plan of an employed family member, Medicare is the secondary payer. This provision applies to group health plans of businesses that employ 100 or more people. Employees of smaller firms and their dependents may also be covered under certain conditions.

Delayed Enrollment Under Medicare Medical Insurance

When you are covered by an employer health plan, you may be able to delay enrollment in Medicare's medical insurance without premium penalty. Your Social Security office can give you more information on special enrollment periods and delayed enrollment in Medicare's medical insurance.

Other Situations Where Medicare Is the Secondary Payer

If you have a work-related illness or injury, services provided as treatment of that illness or injury should be covered by workers' compensation or federal black lung benefits. It is important that your Medicare claim form note that the treatment is related to a work-related illness or injury even if the injury or illness occurred in the past.

Medicare is a secondary payer for up to one year for beneficiaries who are eligible for Medicare solely on the basis of end-stage renal disease, if they have employer group health plan coverage.

Medicare also serves as the secondary payer in cases where automobile medical or no-fault insurance or any liability insurance is available as the primary payer.

Although Medicare benefits are secondary to benefits paid by liability insurers, you must file claims with Medicare first, and Medicare will make a conditional payment. When a liability settlement is reached, Medicare will recover its conditional payments from the settlement amount.

If You Are Entitled to Both Medicare and Veterans Benefits

An individual who is entitled to veterans benefits and to Medicare benefits may choose to receive treatment under either program. Under the law, Medicare cannot pay for services furnished by VA hospitals and VA medical facilities, except for certain emergency hospital services. Also, Medicare cannot pay if the VA has authorized payment for services that a veteran receives in a non-VA hospital or from a non-VA physician. Medicare can pay for covered services a veteran receives from non-VA hospitals and physicians if the VA has not authorized payment for the services.

Since July 1986, the VA has been charging copayments to some veterans with non–service-connected conditions for treatment in a VA hospital or medical facility, or for VA-authorized treatment by non-VA sources. The VA charges copayments when the veteran's income exceeds a particular level. If the VA charges the veteran a copayment for *VA-authorized care by a non-VA physician or hospital,* Medicare may be able to reimburse the veteran, in whole or in part, for his or her VA copayment obligation. But Medicare may not reimburse a veteran for VA copayments for services furnished by VA hospitals and facilities, unless the services are emergency inpatient or outpatient *hospital* services. In the event of the latter, the Medicare payment is subject to both Medicare deductible and coinsurance amounts.

For further information, contact your Medicare intermediary or carrier.

Submitting Claims for a Person Who Dies

When a Medicare beneficiary dies, any hospital insurance payments due will be paid directly to the hospital, skilled nursing facility, home health agency, or hospice that provided covered services.

For services covered under medical insurance, some special rules apply, depending on whether the doctor's or supplier's bill has been paid.

If the bill was paid by the patient or with funds from the patient's estate, payment will be made either to the estate representative or to a surviving member of the patient's immediate family. If someone other than the patient paid the bill, payment may be made to that person.

If the bill has not been paid and the doctor or supplier does not accept assignment, the medical insurance payment can be made to the person who has legal obligation to pay the bill for the deceased patient. The person can claim the medical insurance payment either before or after paying the bill. The Medicare carrier or any Social Security office can provide additional information about how to claim a medical insurance payment after a patient dies.

Time Limits

Under the law, there are some time limits for submitting medical insurance claims. For medical insurance to make payments on your claims, you must send in your claims within these time limits. You always have at least 15 months to submit claims. The following table tells you exactly what the time limits are.

FOR SERVICE YOU RECEIVE BETWEEN	YOUR CLAIM MUST BE SUBMITTED BY
Oct. 1, 1988, & Sept. 30, 1989	Dec. 31, 1990
Oct. 1, 1989, & Sept. 30, 1990	Dec. 31, 1991
Oct. 1, 1990, & Sept. 30, 1991	Dec. 31, 1992

Where to Send Your Claims

The list on pages 145 to 159 gives the names, addresses, and telephone numbers, by state, of the Medicare carriers selected to handle claims. To find out where to send your medical insurance claim, look in the list for the state where you received the services.

Under the name of the state, you will find the name of the carrier that will handle your claim. If there is more than one carrier in the state, look for the county where you received services to find the carrier that will handle your claim. (See page 53 to find out how to submit medical insurance claims.)

If you are not sure where to send your first claim and happen to send it to the wrong place, your claim will be sent to the right place.

Whenever you send in a claim, be sure to include the word "Medicare" in the carrier's address on the envelope. Also, be sure to put your return address and a stamp on the envelope.

After you make a claim, the carrier will usually send you another 1490S form for your next claim. The form will usually show the carrier's name and address in the top right hand corner. If you ever need to file a medical insurance claim and don't have a claim form, you can get one by phoning the Medicare carrier or a Social Security office.

Note: If you are entitled to Medicare under the Railroad Retirement system, send your medical insurance claims to The Travelers Insurance Company office that serves your region. Regional offices of The Travelers are listed in *Your Medicare Handbook for Railroad Retirement Beneficiaries,* which is available at any railroad retirement office.

5

Your Right of Appeal

This chapter tells you about:

If you disagree with a decision on the amount Medicare will pay on a claim or whether services you received are covered by Medicare, you have the right to appeal the decision.

In many instances the first written denial notice you receive will come from the provider of the services (such as a hospital, skilled nursing facility, home health agency, or a hospice). The notice from the provider should explain why it believes Medicare will not pay for the services. You do not have the right to appeal the provider's notice as it is not considered a Medicare decision. If you disagree, ask the provider to file a claim on your behalf to Medicare (which the provider must do), so you can receive a Medicare decision regarding your claim. You then have the right to appeal the Medicare decision if you still disagree.

The notice you receive from Medicare which tells you of the decision made on a claim will also tell you exactly what appeal steps you can take. If you ever need more information about your right to appeal and how to request it, call any Social Security office, the Medicare intermediary or carrier, or the peer review organization in your state. The following is a brief summary of the different Medicare appeals processes.

Appealing Decisions by Peer Review Organizations (PROs)

Peer review organizations (PROs) make decisions on the need for hospital care (see page 10 for a description of PROs). Whenever you are admitted to a Medicare-participating hospital, you will be given "An Important Message from Medicare" (see page 81 for a copy of this message). This briefly describes your rights to a review by the PRO, should the hospital give you a notice of noncoverage. The message includes the name, address, and phone number of the PROs in your state.

Once the PRO makes a determination about your case, you can appeal by requesting a reconsideration if you disagree with the decision of the PRO. Then if you disagree with the PRO's reconsideration decision and the amount in question is $100 or more, you can request a hearing by an administrative law judge. Cases involving $1,000 or more can eventually be appealed to a federal court.

Appealing All Other Hospital Insurance Decisions

Unless you are a member of an HMO or CMP, appeals of decisions on all other services covered under Medicare hospital insurance (skilled nursing facility care, home health care, hospice services, and some inpatient hospital matters not handled by PROs) are handled by Medicare intermediaries. If you disagree with the intermediary's initial decision, you may request a reconsideration. The request can be submitted directly to the intermediary or through your Social Security office. If you disagree with the intermediary's reconsideration decision and the amount in question is $100 or more, you can request a hearing by an administrative law judge. Cases involving $1,000 or more can eventually be appealed to a federal court, after review by the Appeals Council.

Appealing Decisions by Health Maintenance Organizations (HMOs) and Competitive Medical Plans (CMPs)

If you are a member of a Medicare-certified health maintenance organization (HMO) or competitive medical plan (CMP), decisions about coverage and payment for services will usually be made by your HMO/CMP. Your appeal rights are similar to the rights of Medicare beneficiaries under traditional fee-for-service Medicare. Also, federal law requires Medicare-certified HMOs and CMPs to provide a full, written explanation of appeal rights to all members at the time of enrollment, and at least once a year thereafter. If you are a member of such a plan and you have not received a written explanation of your appeal rights, you should request one from your plan's membership office or write to the Health Care Financing Administration.

Appealing Decisions on Medical Insurance Claims

Under Medicare medical insurance, either you, your doctor, your provider, or your supplier submits the claim for payment. Medicare will send you an explanation of the claim decision on a form called "An Explanation of Medicare Benefits" (EOMB). The form also explains how you can appeal denials or payment decisions you disagree with, and gives the name, address, and statewide toll-free number of the carrier (the names and addresses of the carriers and the areas they serve are also listed on pages 145–159 of this book). If you disagree with the decision on your claim, you can ask the carrier to review it. Then if you disagree with the carrier's written explanation of its review decision and the amount in question is $100 or more, you can request a hearing by the carrier. (To reach the $100 amount, you can count other claims that have been reviewed within the past six months.)

If you disagree with the carrier hearing decision and the amount in question is $500 or more, you can request a hearing before an administrative law judge. Cases involving $1,000 or more can eventually be appealed to a federal court, after review by the Appeals Council.

6

What Medicare Does Not Cover

This chapter tells you about:

Care That Is Custodial

Care is considered custodial when it is primarily for the purpose of meeting personal needs and could be provided by persons without professional skills or training. Much of the care provided in nursing homes or by home agencies to persons with chronic, long-term illness or disabilities falls into this category. For example, custodial care includes help in walking, getting in and out of bed, bathing, dressing, eating, and taking medicine. Even if you are in a participating hospital or skilled nursing facility or you are receiving care from a participating home health agency, Medicare does not cover your care if it is mainly custodial.

Care That Is Not Reasonable and Necessary Under Medicare Program Standards

If a doctor places you in a hospital or skilled nursing facility when the kind of care you need could be provided elsewhere, your stay would not be considered reasonable and necessary, so Medicare would not cover your stay. If you stay in a hospital or skilled nursing facility longer than you need to be there, Medicare payments would end when further inpatient care is no longer reasonable and necessary.

If a doctor (or other practitioner) comes to treat you or you visit him or her for treatment more often than is medically necessary, Medicare would not cover the "extra" visits. Medicare cannot cover more services than are reasonable and necessary for your treatment. Any decision of this kind is always based on professional medical advice.

Services Not Covered

This alphabetical list shows most of the major services and supplies not usually paid for by Medicare. However, some of these items can be covered by Medicare under certain conditions described on the pages indicated.

acupuncture

chiropractic services (see page 37)

Christian Science practitioner's services

cosmetic surgery (see page 37)

custodial care

dental care (see page 38)

drugs and medicines you buy yourself with or without a doctor's prescription (see page 31)

eyeglasses and eye examinations for prescribing, fitting, or changing eyeglasses (see page 38)

foot care that is routine (see page 37)

hearing aids and hearing examinations for prescribing, fitting, or changing hearing aids

homemaker services (see page 28)

immunizations (see pages 46–47)

injections that can be self-administered, such as insulin

long-term care (nursing homes)

meals delivered to your home

naturopaths' services

nursing care on full-time basis in your home

orthopedic shoes, unless they are part of a leg brace and are included in the orthopedist's charge

personal convenience items that you request, such as a phone or television in your room at a hospital or skilled nursing facility physical examinations that are routine (for example, yearly physical examinations) and tests directly related to such examinations

private duty nurses

private room (see page 21)

services not reasonable and necessary under Medicare program standards

services payable by another government program

services performed by immediate relatives or members of your household

services provided outside the United States (see page 23)

Limit of Beneficiary Liability

Under Medicare law you will not be held responsible for paying for certain health care services if you could not reasonably be expected to know that the services were not covered by Medicare. This is called limitation of liability, and is often referred to as a "waiver of liability." The waiver applies only when the care is not covered because it was custodial care or was not "reasonable or necessary" under Medicare program standards for diagnosis or treatment. The waiver also applies to denials of home health services where the patient is not homebound, or is not receiving skilled nursing care on an intermittent basis.

7

Getting the Part of Medicare You Do Not Have

This chapter tells you about:

Medical Insurance

If you have Medicare hospital insurance but do not have the medical insurance part of Medicare, you can sign up for medical insurance during the general enrollment period, which is held January 1 through March 31 each year. Your protection will begin July 1 of the year you enroll. If you enroll during a general enrollment period, your monthly premium will be 10% higher than the basic premium for each 12-month period during which you could have had medical insurance but were not enrolled. The basic medical insurance premium through December 31, 1989 was $27.90 a month.

Hospital Insurance

Some individuals 65 or older have Medicare medical insurance but do not meet the requirements for premium-free hospital insurance. If you are in this category, you can get hospital insurance by paying a monthly premium. (This premium applies only to persons who are not entitled to hospital insurance through the Social Security or Railroad Retirement systems or government employment. The basic hospital insurance premium through December 31, 1989 was $156 a month.

You can sign up for premium hospital insurance during the general enrollment period, January 1 through March 31 each year. If you enroll during a general enrollment period that begins more than one year after your 65th birthday, your monthly premium will be 10% higher than the basic premium amount. Your protection will not begin until July 1 of the year you enroll.

For more information about premium amounts, premium surcharges, and how to get the part of Medicare you do not have, contact your Social Security office.

8

Events That Can Change Your Medicare Protection

This chapter tells you about:

When Protection Ends for Persons 65 and Older

If you have Medicare hospital insurance based on your husband's or wife's work record, your protection will end if you and your spouse divorce before your marriage has lasted 10 years. If you have hospital insurance based on your own work record, your protection will continue as long as you live.

Your medical insurance protection will stop if your premiums are not paid or if you voluntarily cancel. If you are thinking about canceling your medical insurance, remember that you may not be able to get private insurance that offers the same protection. Also, if you cancel your medical insurance and then later decide to re-enroll, your premium may be higher and your protection will not begin again until July 1 of the year you re-enroll (unless you qualify for a special enrollment period as described on page 57).

If you are buying Medicare hospital insurance as described previously, you will lose it if you cancel your medical insurance. People who buy hospital insurance must enroll and pay the premium for medical insurance. However, you can cancel hospital insurance and still continue your medical insurance.

If you want more information about canceling your Medicare protection, get in touch with any Social Security office.

When Protection Ends for the Disabled

If you have Medicare because you are disabled, your protection will end if you recover from your disability before you are 65. If you go to work but are still disabled, your Medicare protection may continue for up to 48 months after you begin working.

When Protection Ends for Those with Kidney Failure

If you have Medicare because of permanent kidney failure, your protection will end 12 months after the month the maintenance dialysis treatment stops or 36 months after the month you have a successful kidney transplant.

Your medical insurance protection could stop before that for failure to pay premiums or if you decide to cancel. Call any Social Security office if you ever want to cancel your medical insurance protection.

If you need more information about Medicare coverage of permanent kidney failure, turn to Supplement I, "Medicare Coverage of Kidney Dialysis and Kidney Transplant Services," page 93.

9

Financial Assistance for Low-income Beneficiaries

The Medicare Catastrophic Coverage Act of 1988 provides some limited assistance through Medicaid for paying your share of acute-care costs under Medicare. You must not otherwise be eligible for Medicaid but must meet certain income and resource tests. If your annual income level is below the national poverty level ($5,770 for one person or $7,730 for a family of two, in January 1989) and you do not have access to many financial resources, you *may* qualify for government assistance in paying the Medicare premium, and at least some of the Medicare deductibles and copayments. The maximum annual income level for qualification may vary by state. If you qualify, this financial assistance will be offered through your state's medical assistance (Medicaid) program. The date of availability will vary from state to state. If you think you may qualify, you should contact your state or local welfare, social service, or public health agency.

An Important Message from Medicare

Your Rights While You Are a Medicare Hospital Patient

- You have the right to receive all the hospital care that is necessary for the proper diagnosis and treatment of your illness or injury. According to Federal law, your discharge date must be determined solely by your medical needs, and not by "DRGs" or Medicare payments.
- You have the right to be fully informed about decisions affecting your Medicare coverage and payment for your hospital stay and for any post-hospital services.

- You have the right to request a review by a Peer Review Organization of any written notice of noncoverage that you receive from the hospital stating that Medicare will no longer pay for your hospital care. Peer Review Organizations (PROs) are groups of doctors who are paid by the Federal Government to review medical necessity, appropriateness and quality of hospital treatment furnished to Medicare patients. The phone number and address of the PRO for your area are:

____

____

____

Talk to Your Doctor About Your Stay in the Hospital

You and your doctor know more about your condition and your health needs than anyone else. Decisions about your medical treatment should be made between you and your doctor. **If you have any questions about your medical treatment, your need for continued hospital care, your discharge, or your need for possible post-**

hospital care, don't hesitate to ask your doctor. The hospital's patient representative or social worker will also help you with your questions and concerns about hospital services.

If You Think You Are Being Asked to Leave the Hospital Too Soon

- Ask a hospital representative for a written notice of explanation immediately, if you have not already received one. This notice is called a "notice of noncoverage." You must have this notice of noncoverage if you wish to exercise your right to request a review by the PRO.
- The notice of noncoverage will state either that your doctor or the PRO agrees with the hospital's decision that Medicare will no longer pay for your hospital care.
    - If the hospital and your doctor agree, the PRO does not review your case before a notice of noncoverage is issued. But the PRO will respond to your request for a review of your notice of noncoverage and seek your opinion. You cannot be made to pay for your hospital care until the PRO makes its decision, if you request the review by noon of the first work day after you receive the notice of noncoverage.

- If the hospital and your doctor disagree, the hospital may request the PRO to review your case. If it does make such a request, the hospital is required to send you a notice to that effect. In this situation the PRO must agree with the hospital or the hospital cannot issue a notice of noncoverage. You may request that the PRO reconsider your case after you receive a notice of noncoverage but since the PRO has already reviewed your case once, you may have to pay for at least one day of hospital care before the PRO completes this reconsideration.

IF YOU **DO NOT** REQUEST A REVIEW, **THE HOSPITAL MAY BILL YOU** FOR ALL THE COSTS OF YOUR STAY BEGINNING WITH THE THIRD DAY AFTER YOU RECEIVE THE NOTICE OF NONCOVERAGE. THE HOSPITAL, HOWEVER, CANNOT CHARGE YOU FOR CARE UNLESS IT PROVIDES YOU WITH A NOTICE OF NONCOVERAGE.

How to Request a Review of the Notice of Noncoverage

- If the notice of noncoverage states that your **physician agrees** with the hospital's decision:
    - You must make your request for review to the PRO by **noon of the first work day** after you receive the notice of noncoverage by contacting the PRO by phone or in writing.
    - The PRO must ask for your views about your case before making its decision. The PRO will inform you by phone and in writing of its decision on the review.
    - If the PRO agrees with the notice of noncoverage, you may be billed for all costs of your stay beginning at noon of the day **after** you receive the PRO's decision.

      Thus, you will **not** be responsible for the cost of hospital care before you receive the PRO's decision.
- If the notice of noncoverage states that the **PRO agrees** with the hospital's decision:
    - You should make your request for reconsideration to the PRO **immediately** upon receipt of the notice of noncoverage by contacting the PRO by phone or in writing.

- The PRO can take up to three working days from receipt of your request to complete the review. The PRO will inform you in writing of its decision on the review.
- Since the PRO has already reviewed your case once, prior to the issuance of the notice of noncoverage, the hospital is permitted to begin billing you for the cost of your stay beginning with the third calendar day after you receive your notice of noncoverage **even if the PRO has not completed its review.**
- Thus, if the PRO continues to agree with the notice of noncoverage, **you may have to pay for at least one day of hospital care.**

NOTE: The process described above is called "immediate review." If you miss the deadline for this immediate review while you are in the hospital, you may still request a review of Medicare's decision to no longer pay for your care at any point during your hospital stay or after you have left the hospital. The notice of noncoverage will tell you how to request this review.

Post-Hospital Care

When your doctor determines that you no longer need all the specialized services provided in a hospital, but you still require medical care, he or she may discharge you to a skilled nursing facility or home care. The discharge planner at the hospital will help arrange for the services you may need after your discharge. Medicare and supplemental insurance policies have limited coverage for skilled nursing facility care and home health care. Therefore, you should find out which services will or will not be covered and how payment will be made. Consult with your doctor, hospital discharge planner, patient representative, and your family in making preparations for care after you leave the hospital. **Don't hesitate to ask questions.**

ACKNOWLEDGEMENT OF RECEIPT

My signature only acknowledges my receipt of this Message from (name of hospital) on (date) and does not waive any of my rights to request or make me liable for any payment.

____

Signature of beneficiary or
person acting on behalf of beneficiary

FORM APPROVED
OMB NO. 0938-0008

PATIENT'S REQUEST FOR MEDICAL PAYMENT

IMPORTANT—SEE OTHER SIDE FOR INSTRUCTIONS

PLEASE TYPE OR PRINT INFORMATION

MEDICAL INSURANCE BENEFITS SOCIAL SECURITY ACT

NOTICE: Anyone who misrepresents or falsifies essential information requested by this form may upon conviction be subject to fine and imprisonment under Federal Law. No Part B Medicare benefits may be paid unless this form is received as required by existing law and regulations (20 CFR 422.510).

1	Name of Beneficiary from Health Insurance Card (Last) (First) (Middle)		**SEND COMPLETED FORM TO:**
2	Claim Number from Health Insurance Card	Patient's Sex ☐ Male ☐ Female	
3	Patient's Mailing Address (City, State, Zip Code) Check here if this is a new address ☐ (Street or P.O. Box — Include Apartment Number) (City) (State) (Zip)	3b	Telephone Number (Include Area Code) (___ ___ ___) ___ ___ ___ – ___ ___ ___ ___
4	Describe the Illness or Injury for which Patient Received Treatment	4b	Was condition related to: A. Patient's employment ☐ Yes ☐ No B. Accident ☐ Auto ☐ Other

		4c	Was patient being treated with chronic dialysis or kidney transplant? ☐ Yes ☐ No
5	a. Are you employed and covered under an employee health plan?		☐ Yes ☐ No
	b. Is your spouse employed and are you covered under your spouse's employee health plan?		☐ Yes ☐ No
	c. If you have any medical coverage other than Medicare, such as private insurance, employment related insurance, State Agency (Medicaid), or the VA, complete: Name and Address of other insurance, State Agency (Medicaid), or VA office		
	Policyholders Name:		Policy or Medical Assistance No.
	NOTE: If you DO NOT want payment information on this claim released, put an (X) here ——— ☐		
6	I AUTHORIZE ANY HOLDER OF MEDICAL OR OTHER INFORMATION ABOUT ME TO RELEASE TO THE SOCIAL SECURITY ADMINISTRATION AND HEALTH CARE FINANCING ADMINISTRATION OR ITS INTERMEDIARIES OR CARRIERS ANY INFORMATION NEEDED FOR THIS OR A RELATED MEDICARE CLAIM. I PERMIT A COPY OF THIS AUTHORIZATION TO BE USED IN PLACE OF THE ORIGINAL, AND REQUEST PAYMENT OF MEDICAL INSURANCE BENEFITS TO ME.		
	Signature of Patient (If patient is unable to sign, see Block 6 on reverse)	6b	Date signed

IMPORTANT

ATTACH ITEMIZED BILLS FROM YOUR DOCTOR(S) OR SUPPLIER(S) TO THE BACK OF THIS FORM

Form HCFA-1490S (2-87) DEPARTMENT OF HEALTH AND HUMAN SERVICES—HEALTH CARE FINANCING ADMINISTRATION

Form 1490S—Patient's Request for Medical Payment

HOW TO FILL OUT THIS MEDICARE FORM

Medicare will pay you directly when you complete this form and attach an itemized bill from your doctor or supplier. Your bill does not have to be paid before you submit this claim for payment, but you MUST attach an itemized bill in order for Medicare to process this claim.

FOLLOW THESE INSTRUCTIONS CAREFULLY:

A. Completion of this form.

Block 1.	Print your name shown on your Medicare Card. (Last Name, First Name, Middle Name)
Block 2.	Print your Health Insurance Claim Number including the letter at the end **exactly** as it is shown on your Medicare card. Check the appropriate box for the patient's sex.
Block 3.	Furnish your mailing address and include your telephone number in Block 3b.
Block 4.	Describe the illness or injury for which you received treatment. Check the appropriate box in Blocks 4b and 4c.
Block 5a.	Complete this Block if you are age 65 or older and enrolled in a health insurance plan where you are currently working.
Block 5b.	Complete this Block if you are age 65 or older and enrolled in a health insurance plan where your spouse is currently working.
Block 5c.	Complete this Block if you have any medical coverage other than Medicare. Be sure to provide the Policy or Medical Assistance Number. You may check the box provided if you do not wish payment information from this claim released to your other insurer.
Block 6.	Be sure to sign your name. If you cannot write your name, make an (X) mark. Then have a witness sign his or her name and address in Block 6 too. If you are completing this form for another Medicare patient you should write (By) and sign your name and address in Block 6. You also should show your relationship to the patient and briefly explain why the patient cannot sign.
Block 6b.	Print the date you completed this form.

B. Each itemized bill MUST show all of the following information:

- Date of each service
- Place of each service —Doctor's Office —Outpatient Hospital —Patient's Home —Independent Laboratory —Nursing Home —Inpatient Hospital
- Description of each surgical or medical service or supply furnished.
- Charge for EACH service.

- Doctor's or supplier's name and address. Many times a bill will show the names of several doctors or suppliers. IT IS VERY IMPORTANT THE ONE WHO TREATED YOU BE IDENTIFIED. Simply circle his/her name on the bill.
- It is helpful if the diagnosis is shown on the physician's bill. If not, be sure you have completed Block 4 of this form.
- Mark out any services on the bill(s) you are attaching for which you have already filed a Medicare claim.
- If the patient is deceased please contact your Social Security office for instructions on how to file a claim.
- Attach an Explanation of Medicare Benefits notice from the other insurer if you are also requesting Medicare payment.

COLLECTION AND USE OF MEDICARE INFORMATION

We are authorized by the Health Care Financing Administration to ask you for information needed in the administration of the Medicare program. Authority to collect information is in section 205 (a), 1872 and 1875 of the Social Security Act, as amended.

The information we obtain to complete your Medicare claim is used to identify you and to determine your eligibility. It is also used to decide if the services and supplies you received are covered by Medicare and to insure that proper payment is made.

The information may also be given to other providers of services, carriers, intermediaries, medical review boards, and other organizations as necessary to administer the Medicare program. For example, it may be necessary to disclose information about the Medicare benefits you have used to a hospital or doctor.

With one exception, which is discussed below, there are no penalties under social security law for refusing to supply information. However, failure to furnish information regarding the medical services rendered or the amount charged would prevent payment of the claim. Failure to furnish any other information, such as name or claim number, would delay payment of the claim.

It is mandatory that you tell us if you are being treated for a work related injury so we can determine whether worker's compensation will pay for the treatment. Section 1877 (a) (3) of the Social Security Act provides criminal penalties for withholding this information.

Public reporting burden for this collection of information is estimated to average 16 minutes per response, including the time for reviewing instructions, searching existing data sources, gathering and maintaining the data needed, and completing and reviewing the collection of information. Send comments regarding this burden estimate or any other aspect of this collection of information, including suggestions for reducing this burden to HCFA, P.O. Box 26684, Baltimore, MD 21207; and to the Office of Information and Regulatory Affairs, Office of Management and Budget, Washington, D.C. 20503.

Back Side of Form 1490S

SUPPLEMENT I

Medicare Coverage of Kidney Dialysis and Kidney Transplant Services

Medicare and Treatment for Permanent Kidney Failure

This supplement explains the special rules that apply to Medicare coverage and payment for kidney dialysis and transplant services.

Medicare also pays for a wide range of other health services and supplies. Chapters 2 and 3 of this book describe the other health services and supplies that are covered by Medicare and how payments are made.

Hospital Insurance

Medicare hospital insurance covers medically necessary inpatient hospital care. Under certain conditions, it also covers medically necessary inpatient care in a skilled nursing facility, home health care, and hospice care. The hospital insurance part of Medicare, for example, helps pay for an inpatient stay in an approved hospital for kidney transplant surgery.

Medicare payments for services covered by hospital insurance are made directly to the participating hospital, skilled nursing facility, home health agency, or hospice.

Medical Insurance

Most of the services and supplies needed by people with permanent kidney failure are covered by Medicare medical insurance. For example, medical insurance covers outpatient maintenance dialysis, staff-assisted dialysis, self-dialysis training, and home dialysis.

If you became entitled to Medicare before you developed permanent kidney failure and have not signed up for medical insurance or if your medical insurance has stopped, you can apply for this protection now. If you already have medical insurance but are paying a premium penalty for late enrollment, your premium amount can be reduced to the current basic rate. Get in touch with any Social Security office for more information.

After you have paid $75 in Medicare-approved charges for covered medical expenses in the calendar year, medical insurance generally will pay 80% of the approved charges for any additional covered services you receive during the rest of the year. You are responsible for the remaining 20%.

The first $75 in covered expenses is the medical insurance deductible. You need to meet this $75 deductible only once during the year. The deductible can be met by any combination of covered expenses. You do not have to meet a separate deductible for each different kind of covered service you might receive.

The deductible applies to your expenses related to doctors, providers, and suppliers. Suppliers are persons or organizations other than doctors or health care facilities that furnish equipment or services covered by medical insurance.

When Medicare Protection Begins

When you become entitled to Medicare because of permanent kidney failure, your Medicare protection starts with the third month after the month your course of maintenance dialysis treatments begin. For example, if you begin receiving maintenance dialysis treatments in July, your Medicare coverage would start on October 1.

There are two ways your Medicare protection can begin earlier.

1. Medicare coverage can begin the *first month* of dialysis if you participate in a self-dialysis training program in a Medicare-approved training facility before the third month after dialysis begins, *and* you are expected to complete the training and self-dialyze thereafter.
2. Medicare coverage can begin the month you are admitted to an approved hospital for a kidney transplant or procedures preliminary to a transplant *if* the

transplant takes place in that month or within the two following months. But if the transplant is delayed more than two months after you are admitted to the hospital, Medicare coverage will begin two months before the month the actual transplant takes place, or if earlier, the first day of the third month after maintenance dialysis began.

When Medicare Protection Ends

For people entitled to Medicare *only* because of permanent kidney failure, Medicare protection ends 12 months after the month they no longer require maintenance dialysis treatments or 36 months after the month of a kidney transplant. But if the transplant fails during or after that 36-month period and the person again resumes maintenance dialysis or receives another transplant, Medicare coverage will continue or be reinstated immediately without any waiting period.

Your Medicare medical insurance will stop if you fail to pay premiums or decide to cancel it.

Medicare Payment for Beneficiaries Covered by Employer Group Health Plans

If you become entitled to Medicare *only* because of a permanent kidney failure and are covered by an employer group health plan, Medicare will be the secondary payer during an initial period of up to 12 months. The 12-month period in which Medicare may be secondary begins with the month when regular dialysis starts, or if you become entitled to Medicare because of a kidney transplant, when Medicare protection begins.

Since Medicare entitlement usually begins with the third month after the month in which the individual starts a regular course of dialysis, Medicare is usually the second payer for the last 9 months of the 12-month period. However, for individuals who undertake a course in self-dialysis training or who receive a kidney transplant during the 3-month waiting period, Medicare may be the secondary payer for part or all of this initial 3-month period as well.

Employer plans pay first for kidney treatment and other health services furnished during the 12-month period. However, if the employer plan doesn't pay in full, Medicare may make secondary payments to supplement the amount paid by the employer plan. At the end of the 12-month period, Medicare becomes the primary payer. If you are covered by an employer group health plan during the 12-month period, you should tell the person who furnishes you with medical services so that the services can be billed correctly.

Who Can Provide Maintenance Dialysis and Transplant Surgery

To receive Medicare payments, medical facilities must be specifically approved to provide maintenance dialysis or kidney transplant surgery—even if they already participate in Medicare to provide other health care services covered by the program.

They must meet special health, safety, professional, staffing, and minimum utilization standards directly related to dialysis and kidney transplant services. And they must meet federal, state, and local requirements for medical facility planning.

Your doctor or the facility can tell you whether a facility is approved by Medicare for payment of dialysis and transplant services.

Outpatient Dialysis

Medicare medical insurance helps pay for outpatient maintenance dialysis treatments in any approved dialysis facility. This includes the costs of laboratory tests, equipment, supplies, and other services associated with your treatment. Medical insurance payments for outpatient maintenance dialysis furnished in the facility are always made to the facility.

Medicare pays the facility based on a per-treatment rate that is set in advance. This rate if the facility's *composite rate.* The facility may charge you only 20% of this rate. For example, a typical composite rate might be $130 per treatment. In that case, if you have already met the $75 deductible, medical insurance would pay 80% of $130 (or $104). Medicare *cannot* pay the remaining 20% of the charge (or $26). You are responsible for the 20%.

Occasionally, maintenance peritoneal dialysis treatments extend overnight. These extended peritoneal treatments are covered as outpatient services by medical insurance.

Many of the laboratory tests you receive may be included as part of the facility's maintenance dialysis services. But if you need additional tests, they can be covered as independent laboratory services, outpatient hospital services, or as part of your doctor's services. For more information, see Chapter 3.

Inpatient Dialysis

Generally, maintenance dialysis treatments are covered on an outpatient basis. But if you are admitted to a hospital because your medical condition requires the availability of other specialized hospital services on an inpatient basis, your maintenance dialysis treatments would be covered by hospital insurance as part of the costs of your covered inpatient hospital stay. See Chapter 2 for a detailed explanation of the coverage of inpatient hospital care.

Doctors' Services and Maintenance Dialysis

Doctors' services are covered by Medicare medical insurance. While you are on maintenance dialysis, medical insurance can pay for your doctor's services in the following ways.

Outpatient Maintenance Dialysis

Medicare pays benefits for all physicians' services related to outpatient maintenance dialysis. The Medicare carrier pays for those services through a monthly per-person payment. The same monthly amount is paid for each patient the doctor supervises, regardless of whether the patient dialyzes at home or as an outpatient in an approved dialysis facility. Using this method of physician payment, medical insurance pays 80% of the monthly fee, minus any part of the $75 deductible you have not met. If your doctor accepts assignment, Medicare payment is made directly to him or her; otherwise, you receive the payment.

All services from your doctor that are provided at the time of treatment of your kidney condition are included in the monthly payment. For example, during a visit to your doctor for your kidney condition, you might receive services for bronchitis. All the services you receive during this visit would be included in the monthly payment. But any additional visits for follow-up care of the bronchitis would not be included in the monthly payment. Medical insurance can help pay for additional services of this kind as explained in Chapter 3.

Inpatient Maintenance Dialysis

If you are hospitalized, your doctor has a choice of two methods of payment for furnishing services to you as an inpatient. Your doctor may choose to continue to receive the monthly payment, in which case you cannot be billed for any additional amounts. Or your doctor can choose to bill separately for the inpatient services, which Medicare will pay for in the manner described in Chapter 2. In this case, your doctor's monthly payment will be reduced based on the number of days you are hospitalized.

Self-dialysis Training

Self-dialysis training is covered by Medicare medical insurance on an outpatient basis.

Coverage of self-dialysis training includes your instruction and instruction for the person who will assist you with maintenance self-dialysis at home. Medical insurance also covers the maintenance dialysis treatment and laboratory tests and other services and supplies associated with the treatment.

Medicare *cannot* cover the cost of paid dialysis aides to assist self-dialysis patients at home. Medicare also cannot cover the costs of transportation to and from the outpatient dialysis center, wages that you and your assistant lost while being trained, or the cost of lodging during treatment.

Payment rates for self-dialysis training sessions are higher than those for maintenance dialysis treatments. While charges vary from one dialysis facility to another, depending on the type of facility and its geographic location, a typical charge might be $150 per session. If you had already met the annual deductible, medical insurance would pay 80% of the training rate (or $120). Medicare *cannot* pay the remaining 20% (or $30).

For the services of the doctor who is conducting your self-dialysis training, the maximum total charge medical insurance will approve is $500. If your doctor charges $500, medical insurance would pay 80% of $500 (or $400) if you have already met the deductible. Medicare *cannot* pay the remaining 20% (or $100).

Retraining for self-dialysis—for example, in the use of new equipment—is also covered by Medicare medical insurance on an outpatient basis.

Home Dialysis

Medicare medical insurance covers home dialysis equipment, all necessary supplies, and a wide range of home support services. Home dialysis includes home hemodialysis, home intermittent peritoneal dialysis (IPD), home continuous cycling peritoneal dialysis (CCPD), and home continuous ambulatory peritoneal dialysis (CAPD).

Usually, drugs used in your home are not covered unless a doctor administers them. However, certain drugs for home dialysis patients are covered even though a doctor is not present. The most common of these are heparin, the antidote for heparin when medically indicated, and topical anesthetics. Blood or packed red blood cells *cannot* be covered for home dialysis unless your doctor administers it or personally directs its administration, or if the blood is needed to prime your dialysis equipment (see page 46).

Payment Options Under Home Dialysis

If you dialyze at home, you can choose between two payment options: Method I or Method II, described below. To make a choice, complete the Beneficiary Selection Form HCFA-382, sign it, and return it to the facility supervising your care. Once you make your initial choice, you must continue under that option until December 31 of that year. You can change from one method to the other by filing a new Form 382 at any time, but the change does not go into effect until the following January 1. It is important to remember that choosing Method I or Method II does not in any way prevent you from returning to treatment in a center, selecting another kind of treatment, or choosing to associate with another facility.

Method I: the composite rate. If you choose Method I, your dialysis facility is responsible for providing all services, equipment, and supplies necessary for home dialysis. Medicare pays the facility directly for these items and services at a predetermined composite rate. Under this arrangement, you are responsible for paying the $75 deductible and the 20% coinsurance on the Medicare rate to the facility.

Method II: dealing directly with a supplier. If you choose Method II, you must deal directly with a supplier to obtain your home dialysis equipment or supplies or both. You may obtain from your dialysis facility either your home dialysis equipment or supplies, but not both. While your *facility* must accept assignment (that is, it must accept Medicare's allowance for its charges), your *supplier* may or may not accept assignment. Whether you obtain the items from a supplier or from your facility, you are responsible for any unmet part of the $75 deductible and for 20% coinsurance of the approved charges for these items.

Under *both* methods, you must receive your home dialysis support services from your facility, for which Medicare pays the facility directly.

Home Dialysis Equipment

Under Method I, all home dialysis equipment and equipment-related services are covered under the facility's composite rate payment. Under Method II, medical insurance also covers rental or purchase of dialysis equipment for home use. Delivery, installation, and maintenance charges are included as part of this benefit.

Whether you rent or buy dialysis equipment, medical insurance usually makes monthly payments. If you buy dialysis equipment, the monthly medical insurance payment includes any reasonable interest or carrying charges that may be part of an installment purchase agreement with the supplier of the equipment.

After the $75 deductible, medical insurance pays 80% of the approved monthly rental charge or the approved monthly installment purchase price for your home dialysis equipment.

Medical insurance payments for your home dialysis equipment can continue as long as you need to be dialyzed at home. If your need for home dialysis stops, medical insurance payments also stop. For example, if you no longer need to be dialyzed because you have successful kidney transplant surgery, then medical insurance payments for your home dialysis equipment would usually stop.

If you stop using your home dialysis equipment temporarily—for example, because you are traveling or are hospitalized—medical insurance will continue its payments for the equipment for up to three months after the month in which you last used the equipment. If at a later date you use the equipment again, medical insurance payments would also start again.

Of course, if you purchase your dialysis equipment, medical insurance payments always stop when the purchase price approved as a basis for payments is reached.

Note: Before August 1, 1983, a special rule applied if you obtained your home dialysis equipment from an approved hospital, facility, or nonprofit third-party organization which reserved the equipment for the exclusive use of Medicare patients on home dialysis. If you obtained your equipment under this arrangement, Medicare paid the hospital or facility for the full reasonable cost of the equipment, including installation and maintenance, for as long as you needed it.

Any equipment obtained before August 1, 1983, will still be handled under this special rule. If you have equipment under this rule and choose Method I, your facility's composite rate is reduced by $12 per treatment. Therefore, your coinsurance liability is reduced by 20% of $12, or $2.40. This reduction is made as long as the dialysis machine purchased under this special rule is still in use in your home.

After August 1, 1983, no home dialysis equipment can be purchased under this special rule, but equipment that was purchased and in use before August 1, 1983, can be used by subsequent patients for as long as the equipment lasts.

Home Dialysis Supplies

Medical insurance covers all supplies necessary to perform home dialysis. These include disposable items such as alcohol wipes, sterile drapes, rubber gloves, forceps, scissors, and topical anesthetics. Under Method I, all home dialysis supplies are covered under the facility's composite rate payment, of which the beneficiary is responsible for 20% after the $75 deductible. Under Method II, after the $75 deductible, medical insurance pays 80% of the approved charges for all covered items. Whenever possible, you should accumulate bills until they reach $10 or more before sending in your claim for payment.

Home Dialysis Support Services

Medical insurance covers periodic support services, furnished by an approved hospital or facility, which are necessary to help you remain on home dialysis. After your doctor approves the plan of treatment, such support services may include visits by trained hospital or facility personnel to periodically monitor your home dialysis and to assist in emergencies when necessary. Medical insurance also covers the services of qualified facility or hospital personnel to help with the installation and maintenance of your dialysis equipment and to test and appropriately treat your water supply system.

Under Method I, all home dialysis support services are covered under the facility's composite rate payment, of which the beneficiary is responsible for 20% after the $75 deductible. Under Method II, medical insurance pays directly to the facility 80% of the approved charges for all covered services after the $75 deductible has been met.

Kidney Transplant Surgery

Both parts of Medicare help pay for kidney transplant surgery.

What Hospital Insurance Pays For

Medicare hospital insurance covers your inpatient hospital services in an approved hospital when you are admitted for kidney transplant surgery. Hospital insurance also covers hospital services in preparation for your kidney transplant. This includes the Kidney Registry fee and services such as laboratory and other tests that are required to evaluate your medical condition and the medical conditions of potential kidney donors. These preparatory services are covered whether they are done by the approved hospital where your transplant surgery will take place or by another hospital that participates in Medicare. If there is no kidney donor, the costs of obtaining a suitable kidney for your transplant surgery are also covered.

The inpatient hospital deductible applies only to a beneficiary's first period of hospitalization beginning in a calendar year. After that payment, Medicare will pay for an unlimited number of days a year for covered services.

Hospital insurance pays the full cost of care for a person who donates a kidney for your transplant surgery. This includes all reasonable preparatory, operative, and postoperative recovery expenses connected with the donation. There is no deductible or daily coinsurance amount that you must pay for your donor's hospital stay. The inpatient hospital stay does not qualify your donor for any Medicare benefits not associated with the kidney donation. But Medicare hospital insurance will pay for any additional inpatient hospital care your donor might need if complications result directly from the kidney donation. Medicare does not pay for kidneys; the purchase of human organs is prohibited by law.

Medicare hospital insurance payments are made directly to the hospital.

What Medical Insurance Pays For

Medicare medical insurance covers your surgeon's services for performing the kidney transplant operation. This includes preoperative care, the surgical procedure, and follow-up care. Medical insurance also covers doctors' services provided to your kidney donor during his or her inpatient hospital stay while you are receiving a kidney transplant.

After you meet the $75 medical insurance deductible, medical insurance pays 80 percent of the approved charge for your surgeon's services to you. There is no deductible or coinsurance for doctors' services provided to your kidney donor; Medicare pays these services in full. Medical insurance payments for your surgeon's services are paid for as explained in Chapter 3.

Medicare already pays for your immunosuppressive drugs for a period of one year following your discharge from the transplant hospital. This benefit is subject to the Part B deductible and coinsurance provisions.

How Medicare Pays for Blood

Both parts of Medicare can help pay for whole blood or units of packed red blood cells, blood components, and the cost of blood processing and administration.

If you receive blood as an inpatient of a hospital or skilled nursing facility, hospital insurance can pay all of these blood costs, *except for any nonreplacement fees charged for the first three pints of whole blood or units of packed red cells each year.* The nonreplacement fee is the charge that some hospitals and skilled nursing facilities make for blood that is not replaced.

You are responsible for the nonreplacement fees for the first three pints or units of blood furnished by a hospital or skilled nursing facility. If you are charged nonreplacement fees, you have the option of either paying the fees or having the blood replaced. If you choose to have the blood replaced, you can arrange for another person or a blood assurance plan to replace it for you. A hospital or skilled nursing facility cannot charge you for any of the first three pints of blood you have replaced or have arranged to replace.

Medical insurance can help pay for blood and blood components you receive as an outpatient or as part of other covered services, *except for any nonreplacement fees charged for the first three pints or units received in each calendar year.* After you have met the $75 deductible, medical insurance pays 80% of the approved charges for blood, starting with the fourth pint in a calendar year.

Medicare does not cover blood in connection with self-dialysis at home unless it is provided as part of a doctor's service or is needed solely for the purpose of priming the dialysis equipment.

What Medicare Does Not Cover

The following list shows some of the services and supplies that Medicare does not cover in connection with dialysis and transplant services. Other services and supplies not covered by Medicare are listed on pages 21, 27, 29, 36–37, 40–41, and Chapter 6.

- ambulance or other transportation costs to a facility for routine outpatient maintenance dialysis
- dialysis aides' services to assist in home dialysis
- drugs and medicines you buy yourself with or without a prescription except heparin, the antidote for heparin, topical anesthetics
- inpatient hospital and skilled nursing facility costs when the stay is solely for maintenance dialysis
- lodging costs when an outpatient dialysis facility is not near your home
- wage losses to you and your dialysis partner during self-dialysis training

Other Payment Sources

If you have health care protection from private health insurance, the Veterans Administration, the Indian Health Service, a federal employees' health plan, CHAMPUS, or another source, it also may help pay for services you need for the treatment of permanent kidney failure.

In most states there are agencies that help with some of the medical expenses Medicare does not cover. Some states have Kidney Commissions that assist people in meeting the expenses Medicare cannot pay. And most states have a Medicaid program that helps pay medical expenses in cases of serious financial need.

Under certain circumstances, employer group health plans, including federal employee health plans, will be required to pay their benefits before Medicare pays.

Dialysis Patients Who Travel

If you are a dialysis patient and plan to travel, you should make arrangements for dialysis care along the route of your trip before you travel away from your usual dialysis facility. You are responsible for ensuring that an approved dialysis facility along the way has space and time available for your care, and that the physician and other medical personnel at the facility have enough information about you to treat you properly. Your facility will assist you in furnishing the necessary information.

When you plan your trip, take into account the location of Medicare-approved dialysis facilities. There are over 1,400 facilities around the country. Your facility, dialysis network, or local kidney organization should be able to help you obtain the names and addresses of those facilities.

In general, Medicare will pay only for hospital or medical care received in the United States. An exception is made for emergency care rendered by qualified Canadian or Mexican hospitals (see page 23).

SUPPLEMENT II

Hospice Benefits Under Medicare

Hospice, which is a special way of caring for a patient whose disease cannot be cured, is available as a benefit under Medicare hospital insurance (Part A). Medicare beneficiaries who elect hospice care receive a full range of noncurative medical and support services for their terminal illness while continuing to live in their own homes. This supplement explains the special rules that govern Medicare's coverage of and payment for hospice care.

What Is Hospice Care?

Under Medicare, hospice is primarily a comprehensive home care program that provides all the reasonable and necessary medical and support services for the management of a terminal illness. Covered services include physician services, nursing care, medical appliances and supplies (including outpatient drugs for symptom management and pain relief), home health aide and homemaker services, therapies, medical social services, and counseling. In addition to the broad range of outpatient services, short-term inpatient care is also covered. When a patient receives these services from a Medicare-certified hospice, Medicare hospital insurance pays almost the entire cost. The only expense to the beneficiary is limited cost-sharing for outpatient drugs and inpatient respite care.

Who Is Eligible?

Hospice care is available only if:

- The patient is eligible for Medicare hospital insurance (Part A).
- The patient's doctor and the hospice medical director certify that the patient is terminally ill.
- The patient signs a statement choosing hospice care instead of standard Medicare benefits for the terminal illness.
- The patient receives care from a Medicare-certified hospice program.

Who Can Provide Hospice Care?

Hospice care can be provided by a public agency or private organization that is primarily engaged in furnishing services to terminally ill individuals and their families. To receive Medicare payment, the agency or organization must be certified by Medicare to provide hospice services. Certification is required even if the agency or organization is already approved by Medicare to provide other kinds of health services. A patient can find out whether a hospice program is certified by Medicare by asking his or her physician or checking with the agency or organization offering the program. This information also is available from local Social Security offices.

How Long Can Hospice Care Continue?

Special benefit periods apply to hospice care. A Medicare beneficiary may choose to receive hospice care for two 90-day benefit periods and one subsequent 30-day benefit period for a total of 210 days. Regardless of whether they are used one right after the other or at different times, the patient must be certified as terminally ill at the beginning of each benefit period.

A patient choosing hospice care may change hospice programs once each benefit period. A patient also has the right to cancel hospice care at any time and return to standard Medicare coverage. If cancellation is made before the end of either 90-day benefit period, any days left in the period are lost, but the patient is still eligible for the remaining benefit periods. For example: If a patient cancels at the end of 60 days in the first 90-day benefit period, the remaining 30 days in the period are forfeited. However, the patient is still eligible for the second 90-day period and the 30-day period. If cancellation occurs during or after the 30-day benefit period, the patient cannot use the hospice benefit again.

How Is Payment Made?

Medicare pays the hospice directly at specified rates depending on the type of care given each day. The patient is responsible only for the following copayments:

- Drugs or biologicals: The hospice can charge 5% of the reasonable cost, up to a maximum of $5, for each prescription for outpatient drugs or biologicals for pain relief and symptom management.
- Respite care: The hospice may periodically arrange for inpatient care for the patient to give temporary relief to the person who regularly provides care in the home. Respite care is limited each time to stays of no more than five days. The patient can be charged about $3.25 a day for each day of respite care. The charge varies slightly depending on the geographic area of the country.

Are Other Medicare Benefits Available in Addition to Hospice Care?

When a Medicare beneficiary chooses hospice care, he or she gives up the right to standard Medicare benefits for treatment of the terminal illness. Medicare pays the entire cost of the covered services required to manage the illness, except for the copayments for respite care and outpatient prescription drugs and biologicals. A hospice patient can, however, qualify for standard Medicare benefits if:

- The patient has Medicare medical insurance (Part B)

and the patient's attending physician is not working for the hospice. In that case, Medicare Part B will help pay for the physician's services. Medicare pays 80% of the approved amount for covered services after the patient meets the Part B annual deductible of $75.

- The patient requires covered Medicare services for the treatment of a condition unrelated to the terminal illness.

All services required for treatment of the terminal illness must be provided by or through the hospice. When a Medicare beneficiary chooses hospice care, Medicare will not pay for:

- treatment for the terminal illness which is not for symptom management and pain control
- care provided by another hospice that was not arranged by the patient's hospice
- care from another provider which duplicates care the hospice is required to provide.

SUPPLEMENT III

Medicare and Employer Health Plans

Am I Entitled to an Employer Heath Plan?

- If You Are Age 65 or Older . . . and you are working, or you have a spouse, any age, who works, and your or your spouse's firm has 20 or more employees, you must be offered the same health insurance benefits that the employer offers younger workers and spouses. (This also applies if you or your spouse is self-employed and covered by a plan through connection with a firm that has 20 or more employees.)*
- If You Are Under Age 65 . . . and you are entitled to Medicare based on disability, and you or a member of

*This description of employer health plan coverage does not apply to Medicare beneficiaries who have permanent kidney failure. Individuals under age 65 with permanent kidney failure who have employer group health plan coverage should consult Supplement I on page 93.

your family works for an employer who has 100 or more employees, the employer must offer you the same health insurance benefits offered to employees who are not entitled to Medicare.*

Must I Accept the Employer Plan?

You may accept or reject the plan offered by your employer or your spouse's employer. If you accept the employer plan, it will be your primary plan.

If you don't accept your or your spouse's employer plan, Medicare is your primary payer. This also applies to disabled individuals who do not accept their own or a family member's plan. But if you make that choice, the employer plan cannot pay supplemental benefits for Medicare-covered services. You must buy your own supplemental health insurance or "Medigap" plan, if you feel you need such additional protection.

Even if you don't accept your or your spouse's employer plan and Medicare is your primary payer, your employer or your spouse's employer can offer health insurance protection for health care services that are not covered by Medicare (such as hearing aids or routine dental care).

What Is a Primary Plan?

A primary health insurance plan is one that pays first for any covered health care services you receive. For example, if you or your spouse is age 65 or older and working and you are covered by an employer plan and by Medicare, your employer plan is the primary payer. Medicare is the secondary payer.

If I Accept the Employer Plan, How Does It Affect My Medicare Coverage?

If your employer plan does not pay all the charges, Medicare may pay secondary benefits for Medicare-covered services. In other words, it can help pay some of the expenses not paid by the employer plan. If you are not already entitled to Medicare hospital insurance (Medicare Part A), you should apply for it. It can supplement your employer plan.

Whether you wish to enroll in or keep Medicare medical insurance (Medicare Part B) will depend on how fully the employer plan covers the doctors' and other health services that Medicare medical insurance covers. You need to consider whether the secondary benefits Medicare medical insurance would pay are worth the cost to you.

Isn't There a Penalty for Signing up Late for Medicare Medical Insurance?

Not in all cases. If you are covered under an employer plan from the time you are first eligible for Medicare, special rules give you seven months to enroll in Medicare medical insurance beginning when the employee stops working or drops the employer plan, whichever occurs first. However, if you expect work to stop or the employer plan coverage to end with the month you reach age 65 or any of the three following months, you should inquire immediately at your Social Security office to find out about enrolling in Medicare medical insurance.

What Do I Do About Filing Claims If I Have Employer Plan Coverage?

Claims should be filed first with the employer's group health plan and then with Medicare.

You should give the hospital, doctor, and any other supplier of covered services the necessary information about the employer plan (name, policy number, etc.) and inform them that the employer plan should be billed first.

If, for any reason, your doctor or supplier does not submit claims to the employer plan, send your own claim first to the employer plan or ask your personnel office to assist you. If the employer plan does not pay in full for services Medicare covers, enclose a copy of the employer plan explanation of benefits with your claim to Medicare for secondary benefits.

To Find Out More

If you have questions or need additional advice about Medicare eligibility or benefits, contact your nearest Social Security office or the Medicare insurance carrier that handles your Medicare claims. (If you're entitled to Medicare under the Railroad Retirement system, contact your nearest Railroad Retirement Board district office.) For information on your private group plan coverage, consult your employer or your spouse's employer.

SUPPLEMENT **IV**

Medicare and Prepayment Plans

Today, more than ever, Medicare beneficiaries have an increasing variety of quality health care sources to choose from. Among them are the growing number of **prepayment health plans,** including **health maintenance organizations (HMOs)** and **competitive medical plans (CMPs),** which have contracts with the federal government to provide services to Medicare beneficiaries. The following should answer most of your questions regarding the advantages and limitations of receiving your care through HMOs and CMPs.

Prepayment plans might be thought of as a combination insurance company and doctor/hospital. Like an insurance company, they cover health care costs in return for a monthly premium, but like a doctor or hospital, they furnish actual health care. Since they provide health care for a fixed prepaid amount, they have an incentive to keep costs as low as possible. This supplement describes prepayment plans that have contracts with Medicare.

What Services Do Prepayment Plans Offer?

Prepayment plans with Medicare contracts must offer at least all the services covered by Medicare that are generally available in their area. (For a list of covered Medicare services, see Chapters 2 and 3.) Under a Medicare contract with a prepayment plan, Medicare pays the plan a monthly amount for the cost of covered Medicare services *less* deductibles and coinsurance. Therefore, you may be required to pay the plan a monthly premium that covers the cost of deductibles and coinsurance.

Also, prepayment plans may offer services above and beyond those covered by Medicare. Some of these services may be offered free of additional charge (over and above the premium that covers normal Medicare deductible and coinsurance amounts). Some services may be offered for an additional charge. When you enroll, the plan must tell you what part of its charges covers the Medicare deductible and coinsurance and what part, if any, is for services not paid for by Medicare.

There are two basic types of prepayment plans:

- Those operating at one or more centralized locations
- Those operating through individual doctors' offices

If you live in an area that is served by more than one prepayment plan, you should compare benefits and costs to determine which plan best suits your needs.

Must I Continue to Pay the Medicare Part B Medical Insurance Premium?

Yes, you're required to have and pay for Part B of Medicare to be a Medicare member of a prepayment plan.* This premium, which you pay to the government, establishes your entitlement to Part B services whether or not you join a prepayment plan.

For most people, this premium will continue to be deducted from their monthly Social Security checks. The premium you pay the prepayment plan is for deductibles and coinsurance, and for benefits in addition to those covered by Medicare. It is *not* the premium for Medicare Part B medical insurance.

Are There Other Requirements to Join a Prepayment Plan?

Yes. For example, you must:

- Live in the area served by the plan under its Medicare contract
- Have Medicare Part B medical insurance
- Agree to follow the prepayment plan's rules

*If you are over age 65 and you are a member of an HMO or CMP *through your employer*, you are *not* required to keep and pay for Part B of Medicare. Check with your personnel office or the Social Security office for more details.

- Not be entitled to Medicare coverage because of kidney failure requiring dialysis or a kidney transplant
- Not be receiving hospice care

Will I Always Have the Same Doctor?

When you enroll, most prepayment plans allow you to select a doctor from those who are part of the plan. When you make an appointment, you usually will see the doctor you've selected. However, if you need to see a doctor quickly and your selected doctor is busy, you may see another plan doctor. Also, you may change doctors within the plan, if you desire.

What About Specialists and Hospital Care?

Many plans will employ a full assortment of medical specialists. However, if you need a specialist that is not available at the plan for a covered Medicare service, the plan will arrange for the appointment and pay the specialist. Similarly, if you need hospitalization and the plan does not have its own hospital, it will make all arrangements for your care. Since the plan arranges for all your health care, it has your complete medical records, which it will make available to the doctor treating you. If you get sick away from home, the HMO/CMP pays for any emergency or urgently needed medical care.

Why Join a Prepayment Plan?

People join prepayment plans for a variety of reasons. Some of the most frequently mentioned are:

- Various kinds of care needed are available in one place (for example, doctors' services, hospital care, laboratory tests, X-rays, etc.).
- A fixed monthly payment makes budgeting of total health care expenses easier.
- There's no need to pay each time you need a service (this is true for most plans, although some may charge a nominal fee for individual services).
- Benefits beyond those covered by Medicare are available for no additional charge at some plans.
- Emergency care is available 24 hours a day, seven days a week.
- There's no paperwork or claim forms to fill out.

Prepayment plans try to save you money by treating illness early and helping you stay healthy, thus reducing the potential for expensive and inconvenient hospital stays.

Are There Any Other Factors to Consider?

When deciding whether to enroll in a prepayment plan, consider whether the plan is in a location convenient to you and whether adequate transportation is available to get you to the plan. Consider, too, that if you receive services outside the plan system, you may pay additional fees.

Medicare pays some plans for *all* your covered health care costs. Services received outside these plans, other than emergency or urgently needed services, are not paid for separately by Medicare.

If you have a long-standing and satisfactory relationship with your present doctor, you may not wish to change to a prepayment plan doctor and a new way of obtaining health care which uses auxiliary personnel and a staff larger than the traditional, more intimate private practice. Consider all these factors in deciding whether a prepayment plan will be of benefit to you.

What If the Prepayment Plan Won't Pay for Necessary Care?

If the plan issues a denial for payment of any service, and you strongly believe it should pay, you have the same appeal rights as under the regular Medicare program. These rights are explained in Chapter 5.

If you ever decide for any reason that you no longer want to be a member of the plan, you are free to disenroll.

To Find Out More

For more information about health maintenance organizations and competitive medical plans, contact your local Social Security office. Its staff can tell you about any prepayment plans with Medicare contracts in your area and how to get more specific information about them.

SUPPLEMENT V

Guide to Health Insurance for People with Medicare

Some Basic Things You Should Know

Medicare pays a large part of your health care expenses, but it does not pay them all. There are limits on Medicare payments for some covered services and medical supplies. You also must pay certain amounts called deductibles and copayments.

Some services are not covered either by Medicare or most private insurance. For example:

- Custodial care in a nursing home or at home is not covered by Medicare or most private insurance policies on the market today (see page 135).
- Medicare and most private health insurance policies pay only a specified percent of the amount approved by Medicare. You pay the rest, including any charges

in excess of those approved by Medicare. To avoid extra charges, ask your doctors and medical suppliers, such as laboratories and therapists, whether they participate in Medicare or accept assignment of Medicare benefits. Assignment means that your doctor or other medical supplier has agreed to bill Medicare and accept the amount approved by Medicare as the total payment for services and supplies covered by the program. Participating doctors and suppliers accept assignment on all Medicare claims (see page 49).

- Insurance to supplement Medicare, commonly called **supplemental health insurance,** or **Medigap** insurance, is not sold or serviced by federal or state governments. Do not believe advertising or agents who suggest that Medicare supplement insurance is a government-sponsored program.

Before you consider buying insurance to supplement Medicare, you should know what Medicare benefits are. Chapter 2 and 3 of this book explain the specific services covered and not covered by Medicare; Chapter 6 summaries the services not covered. Please review these chapters carefully.

Do You Need Private Health Insurance in Addition to Medicare?

Not everyone does.

- If you are a Medicare beneficiary enrolled in a prepayment plan, such as a health maintenance organization (HMO) or competitive medical plan (CMP), which has a contract with Medicare, you may not need a Medicare supplement policy (see page 133).

- Low-income people who are eligible for Medicaid generally do not need additional insurance. Individuals who are eligible for regular Medicaid benefits qualify for certain health care benefits beyond those covered by Medicare, such as long-term nursing home care.

- The Medicare Catastrophic Coverage Act of 1988 provides some limited financial assistance through Medicaid for paying your share of acute care costs if you are not otherwise eligible for Medicaid and you meet certain income and resource tests. If your annual income level is below the national poverty level ($5,770 for one person or $7,730 for a family of two) and you do not have access to many financial resources, you may qualify for government assistance in paying the Medicare premium, and at least some of the Medicare deductibles and copayments. The maximum annual income for qualification may vary by state. If you qualify, this financial assistance will be offered through your state's medical assistance (Medicaid) program. If you think you may qualify, you should contact your state or local social service agency.

- Whether you need health insurance in addition to Medicare is a decision you should discuss with someone you know who understands insurance and your financial situation. The best time to do this is before you reach age 65.

Types of Private Health Insurance

Private health insurance is available through group and individual policies. It is offered by some companies through agents and by other companies directly through advertising media and mail. The value and extent of coverage differs widely among both group and individual policies.

Types of Individual and Group Health Insurance Coverages

Medicare supplement insurance. Supplemental insurance pays some or all of Medicare's deductibles and copayments. Some policies may also pay for some health services not covered by Medicare. The National Association of Insurance Commissioners (NAIC) has revised its model regulation to include new minimum benefit standards for Medicare supplement policies. It requires that as a minimum benefit, Medicare supplement policies include:

- Coverage of all or none of the Medicare Part A deductible, which is $592 in 1990.
- Coverage for the blood deductible under Part A, unless the blood is replaced.
- Coverage for the 20% copayment under Medicare Part B up to $5,000 after you pay Medicare's $75 deductible, and the first $125 of Medicare copayments.

To determine when revised minimum benefit standards go into effect in your state, consult your state insurance department (see pages 161–172).

Some policies may also pay for some health services not covered by Medicare. Medicare pays only for services that are determined to be medically necessary and only the amount Medicare determines to be reasonable (see page 142). Most Medicare supplement policies do not pay for services Medicare finds unnecessary, or for charges in excess of Medicare's approved amount.

Prepayment plans. There may be one or more prepayment plans such as a health maintenance organization (HMO) or competitive medical plan (CMP) in your area which participate in the Medicare program. Prepayment plans both insure health care and provide health care services. People who join are required to receive health services directly from physicians and other providers affiliated with the plan, except in an emergency. Be aware, however, that as a Medicare beneficiary you are not eligible for enrollment in a prepayment plan unless you reside in the plan's service area and are enrolled in Medicare Part B. If you enroll in a prepayment plan, Medicare pays the plan a fixed amount each month to provide you with all Medicare-approved services. You may be required to pay the plan a monthly premium that covers the cost of deductibles and copayments that would be your responsibility under Medicare if you were not a member of a prepayment plan. However, depending on the plan, there may not be an extra premium and the plan may offer services beyond those covered by Medicare. Services are prepaid, so there are usually no claim forms to process. If you enroll in a prepayment plan, you may not need

Medicare supplement insurance. See Supplement IV for more information.

Group Insurance

Employer group insurance. Many people are covered by a group plan while they are employed. Find out before you retire whether your group coverage can be continued or converted to a suitable individual Medicare supplement policy when you reach age 65. Check carefully the price and the benefits, including benefits for your spouse. Employer group insurance that is continued or converted after retirement usually has the advantage of having no waiting periods or pre-existing-condition exclusions. Consult your employer for information about special rules that apply to employer group coverage for people who continue to work after they reach age 65.

If you are 65 or older and insured by an employer health plan either through your current employment or the current employment of a spouse of any age, you have the choice of using either the employer plan (if the employer has at least 20 employees) or Medicare as your primary health insurance. If you choose the employer plan, it will be the primary payer of your hospital and medical bills and Medicare will be the secondary payer. In other words, if your employer plan does not pay all of the charges, Medicare may pay some of the charges for Medicare-covered services. If you do not choose your (or your spouse's) employer plan, Medicare will become the primary payer of any covered health services you receive. If you choose Medicare as the primary payer, you must so notify your employer, and the employer plan is not permitted to pay supplemental benefits for Medicare-covered services. However, your employer may offer a plan that pays for health care services not covered by Medicare, such as hearing aids and routine dental care. For more information on employer health plans, see Supplement III.

Association group insurance. Many organizations other than employers offer various kinds of group health insurance coverage to their members over age 65. Beware of claims of low group rates, because coverage under group policies may be as expensive or more costly than comparable coverage under individual policies. Be sure you understand the benefits included and then compare prices.

Other Types of Coverage

The following types of coverage are generally limited in scope and are not substitutes for Medicare supplement insurance, prepayment plans, or long-term-care insurance.

Nursing home coverage. Most people who enter nursing homes do so to receive custodial care, which is not covered by Medicare or most Medicare supplement policies. The only care in nursing homes that Medicare covers is skilled nursing care or skilled rehabilitative care which is provided in a skilled nursing facility (SNF). (See page 24 for a description of skilled nursing facility care.) To qualify for Medicare coverage for skilled nursing facility care, your primary need must be for daily skilled nursing or skilled rehabilitative therapy at least five times a week. The daily skilled services must be ones which, as a practical matter, can be provided only on an inpatient basis. The services must also be provided in a Medicare-certified skilled nursing facility. Medicare also requires a three-day prior hospital stay in order for a stay in a skilled nursing facility to be covered. (See pages 132–133 for a discussion of new minimum benefit standards for Medicare supplement policies.) While skilled nursing facility coverage was not required, it was included in some Medicare supplement policies. Those policies usually pay only the copayments associated with days of care Medicare pays for.

When Medicare coverage for skilled nursing facility care ends because the patient no longer requires this level or intensity of care, coverage under existing (pre-1989) Medicare supplement policies usually also stops. This may also be the case for policies issued under the new minimum benefit standards.

There are, however, insurance policies you can buy to cover custodial care, care in an intermediate care facility (ICF), or skilled nursing facility care beyond that covered by Medicare. One such policy is a long-term-care policy. Many new long-term-care insurance products have been coming onto the market in the last few years. Some of these offer considerably better coverage than the older types of nursing home insurance which used to be the only coverage available. Some of the newer types of long-term-care policies will also cover some in-home care beyond that which Medicare provides under the Home Health benefit.

If you are in the market for nursing home coverage or long-term-care insurance, be sure you know which types of nursing homes and services are covered by the different policies available, by Medicare, and by any Medicare supplement insurance you may have. If you purchase nursing home or long-term-care insurance (or have existing nursing home coverage), you should make sure that you are not duplicating skilled nursing facility coverage provided by any Medicare supplement policy or prepayment plan coverage you may have.

Hospital confinement indemnity coverage. This pays a fixed amount for each day you are hospitalized up to a designated number of days. Some coverage may have added benefits such as surgical benefits or skilled nursing home confinement benefits.

Specified disease coverage. (not available in some states) provides benefits for only a single disease, such as cancer, or a group of specified diseases. The value of such coverage depends on the chance you will get the specific disease or diseases covered. Benefits are usually limited to payment of a fixed amount for each type of treatment. Benefits are not designed to fill the Medicare gaps.

Shopping for Private Health Insurance

- **Shop carefully before you buy.** Policies differ widely as to coverage and cost, and companies differ as to service. Contact different companies and compare the policies carefully before you buy.
- **Don't buy more policies than you need.** Duplicate coverage is costly and not necessary. A single com-

prehensive policy is better than several policies with overlapping or duplicate coverages

- **Consider your alternatives.** To better meet your health care needs, consider continuing the group coverage you have at work; joining an HMO, CMP, or other prepayment plan; buying a long-term-care insurance policy; or buying a Medicare supplement policy.
- **Check for pre-existing-condition exclusions.** These reduce or eliminate coverage for existing health conditions. Many policies exclude coverage for pre-existing health conditions. Pre-existing conditions are generally defined as those conditions for which medical advice was given or treatment was recommended by or received from a physician before the effective date of your coverage under an insurance policy.

  Most state laws require Medicare supplement policies to cover pre-existing conditions after the policy has been in effect six months.

  Don't be misled by the phrase "no medical examination required." If you have had a health problem, the insurer might not cover you for expenses connected with that problem.
- **Beware of replacing existing coverage.** Be suspicious of a suggestion that you give up your policy and buy a replacement. Often the new policy will impose waiting periods or will have exclusions or waiting periods for pre-existing conditions covered by your current policy. On the other hand, don't keep inadequate policies simply because you have had them a long time. You don't get credit with a company just because you've paid many years for a policy.

- **Be aware of maximum benefits.** Most policies have some type of limit on benefits, which may be expressed in terms of dollars payable or the number of days for which payment will be made. Keep in mind that some insurance policies pay less than the Medicare-approved amount (or nothing) for hospital outpatient medical services or services in a doctor's office.

- **Check your right to renew.** Beware of policies that let the company refuse to renew your policy on an individual basis. These policies provide the least permanent coverage.

  Most policies cannot be canceled by the company unless all policies of that type are canceled in the state. Therefore, these policies cannot be canceled because of claims or disputes. Some policies are guaranteed renewable for life. This means that although your insurance premiums may be adjusted from time to time, the insurance company cannot cancel your coverage. Policies that can be renewed automatically offer added protection.

- **Be aware that policies to supplement Medicare are neither sold nor serviced by the state or federal governments.** State insurance departments approve policies sold by insurance companies, but approval means only that the company and policy meet requirements of state law. Do not believe statements that insurance to supplement Medicare is a government-sponsored program. If anyone tells you that he or she is from the government and later tries to sell you an insurance policy, report that person to your state insurance department or federal authorities (see pages 161–172). This type of representation is a violation of federal and state law. It is also unlawful for a company or agent to falsely claim that a policy has been approved for sale in any state in which it has not received state approval, or to use fraudulent means to gain approval.

- **Know with whom you're dealing.** A company must meet certain qualifications to do business in your state. This is for your protection. Agents also must be licensed by your state and may be required by the state to carry proof of licensure showing their name and the company they represent. If the agent cannot verify that he or she is licensed, do not buy from that person. A business card is not a license.
- **Keep agents' and/or companies' names, addresses, and telephone numbers.** Write down the agents' and/or companies' names, addresses, and telephone numbers, or ask for a business card that provides all that information.
- **Take your time.** Do not let a short enrollment period put pressure on you. Professional salespeople will not rush you. If you question whether a program is worthy, ask the salesperson to explain it to a friend or relative whose judgment you respect. Allow yourself time to think through your decision.

If You Decide to Buy

- **Complete the application carefully.** Some companies ask for detailed medical information. If they do and you omit the requested medical information, the company can refuse coverage for an omitted condition for a period of time or it may deny a claim and/or cancel your policy. Do not believe anyone who tells you that your medical history on an application is not important.

- **Look for an outline of coverage.** You should be given a clearly worded summary of the policy. *Read it carefully.*
- **Do not pay cash.** Pay by check, money order, or bank draft made payable to the insurance company, not to the agent or anyone else.
- **Check for a "free-look" provision.** New standards require insurance companies to give you at least 30 days to review a Medicare supplement policy. If you decide you don't want the policy, send it back to the agent or company within 30 days of receiving it and you will be entitled to a refund of all premiums you paid. Contact your state insurance department if you encounter a problem in obtaining a refund.
- **Policy delivery or refunds should be prompt.** The insurance company should deliver a policy within 30 days. If it does not, contact the company and obtain in writing a reason for the delay. If 60 days go by without information, contact your state insurance department.
- **For your protection.** Federal criminal and civil penalties as well as state penalties can be imposed against any company or agent who knowingly sells you a health insurance policy that substantially duplicates coverage you already have, but will not pay benefits if your medical expenses are covered by another in-

surance policy or Medicare. There are also penalties for claiming that a policy meets legal standards for certification when it does not, and for using the mail for delivery of advertisements of Medicare supplement health insurance policies that have not been approved for sale in a state. It is also unlawful for a company or agent to suggest that it represents the Medicare program or any government agency. If you believe you have been the victim of these or any other illegal sales practices, you should contact your state insurance department (see pages 161–172) or call the toll-free hotline maintained by the U.S. Department of Health and Human Services: 1-800-888-1998.

You should also report the misuse by any individual or company of the names, letters, symbols or emblems of the U.S. Department of Health and Human Services, the Social Security Administration, or Health Care Financing Administration. A new Federal law prohibits the use of these agencies' identifying marks and names or variations of them to falsely claim or suggest that they have approved, endorsed or authorized any item, including insurance policies.

Approved Amount

In deciding whether a charge is "reasonable," Medicare reviews each year the usual charges of doctors and suppliers for each covered service and the charges of other doctors and suppliers in the area for the same service. The amount approved in payment for a claim is often lower than the actual charge made by the doctor or supplier.

Many Medicare supplement insurance policies pay only the Medicare copayment that you are responsible for; that is, 20% of Medicare's approved amount. You might not get 100% coverage for your Part B bills even if you have Medicare Part B and private insurance. Here's how this could happen:

Suppose your doctor charges you $400 for an operation and Medicare determines the approved amount to be $300. Assuming you have already met the annual Part B deductible, Medicare would pay 80% of the $300, or $240. Most insurance policies would pay 20% of the $300, or $60. You would pay $100—the difference between your doctor's actual charge and Medicare's approved amount. However, you may avoid this extra payment if your doctor accepts assignment (see page 49).

Paying for Medicare

Part A is financed through part of the Social Security (FICA) tax paid by all workers and their employers. You do not have to pay a monthly premium for Medicare Part A if you or your spouse is entitled to benefits under either the Social Security or Railroad Retirement systems, or worked a sufficient period of time in federal, state, or local government employment to be insured. Some disabled persons who do not meet the age requirement of 65 may also qualify for benefits. If you do not meet the qualifications for Part A benefits, you may purchase the coverage if you are at least 65 years old. The monthly premium is estimated at $175 in 1990.

For Additional Help

If you need additional help or advice on Medicare benefits or eligibility, contact your nearest Social Security office or the Medicare insurance carrier in your area.

For information on private insurance to supplement Medicare, check your state insurance department or state agency on aging. (See the lists on pages 161–185.)

If you bought or are considering buying a health insurance policy, the company or its agent should answer your questions. If you do not get the service you feel you deserve, discuss the matter with your state insurance department.

Medicare Carriers State by State

Note: The toll-free or 800 numbers listed below can be used only in the states or service areas indicated. Also listed are the local commercial numbers for some carriers.

ALABAMA
Medicare/Blue Cross-Blue Shield of Alabama
P.O. Box C-140
Birmingham, AL 35283
1-800-292-8855
205-988-2244

ALASKA
Medicare/Aetna Life & Casualty
200 S.W. Market St., P.O. Box 1998
Portland, OR 97207-1998
1-800-547-6333

ARIZONA
Medicare/Aetna Life & Casualty
P.O. Box 37200
Phoenix, AZ 85069

1-800-352-0411
602-861-1968

ARKANSAS
Medicare/Arkansas Blue Cross & Blue Shield
A Mutual Insurance Company
P.O. Box 1418
Little Rock, AR 72203
1-800-482-5525
501-378-2320

CALIFORNIA
Counties of: Los Angeles, Orange, San Diego, Ventura, Imperial, San Luis Obispo, Santa Barbara
Medicare/Transamerica Occidental Life Insurance Co.
Box 50061
Upland, CA 91785-0061
1-800-252-9020
213-748-2311

Rest of state: Medicare Claims Dept.
Blue Shield of California
Chico, CA 95976

In area codes 209, 408, 415, 707, 916:
1-800-952-8627
916-743-1583

In area codes 213, 619, 714, 805, 818:
1-800-848-7713
714-824-0900

COLORADO
Medicare/Blue Shield of Colorado
700 Broadway
Denver, CO 80273
1-800-332-6681
303-831-2661

CONNECTICUT

Medicare/The Travelers Insurance Co.
P.O. Box 5005
Wallingford, CT 06493-5005
1-800-982-6819

In Hartford: 203-728-6783

DELAWARE

Medicare/Pennsylvania Blue Shield
P.O. Box 65
Camp Hill, PA 17011
1-800-851-3535

DISTRICT OF COLUMBIA

Medicare/Pennsylvania Blue Shield
P.O. Box 100
Camp Hill, PA 17011
1-800-233-1124

FLORIDA

Medicare/Blue Shield of Florida, Inc.
P.O. Box 2525
Jacksonville, FL 32231
1-800-333-7586
904-355-3680

GEORGIA

Medicare/Aetna Life & Casualty
P.O. Box 3018
Savannah, GA 31402-3018
1-800-727-0827
912-927-0934

HAWAII
Medicare/Aetna Life & Casualty
P.O. Box 3947
Honolulu, HI 96812
1-800-272-5242
808-524-1240

IDAHO
Equicor, Inc.
P.O. Box 8048
Boise, ID 83707
1-800-632-6574
208-342-7763

ILLINOIS
Medicare Claims
Blue Cross & Blue Shield of Illinois
P.O. Box 4422
Marion, IL 62959
1-800-642-6930
312-938-8000

INDIANA
Medicare Part B
Associated Insurance Companies, Inc.
P.O. Box 7073
Indianapolis, IN 46207
1-800-622-4792
317-842-4151

IOWA
Medicare/Blue Shield of Iowa
636 Grand
Des Moines, IA 50309

1-800-532-1285
515-245-4785

KANSAS

Counties of: Johnson, Wyandotte
Medicare/Blue Shield of Kansas City
P.O. Box 169
Kansas City, MO 64141
1-800-892-5900
816-561-0900

Rest of state: Medicare/Blue Shield of Kansas
P.O. Box 239
Topeka, KS 66601
1-800-432-3531
913-232-3773

KENTUCKY

Medicare-Part B
Blue Cross & Blue Shield of Kentucky
100 East Vine St.
Lexington, KY 40507
1-800-432-9255
606-233-1441

LOUISIANA

Blue Cross & Blue Shield of Louisiana Medicare Administration
P.O. Box 95024
Baton Rouge, LA 70895-9024
1-800-462-9666

In New Orleans: 504-529-1494
In Baton Rouge: 504-272-1242

MAINE
Medicare/Blue Shield of
Massachusetts/Tri State
P.O. Box 1010
Biddeford, ME 04005
1-800-492-0919

MARYLAND
Counties of: Montgomery, Prince Georges
Medicare/Pennsylvania Blue Shield
P.O. Box 100
Camp Hill, PA 17011
1-800-233-1124

Rest of state: Maryland Blue Shield, Inc.
700 E. Joppa Road
Towson, MD 21204
1-800-492-4795
301-561-4160

MASSACHUSETTS
Medicare/Blue Shield of Massachusetts, Inc.
55 Accord Park Drive
Rockland, MA 02371
1-800-882-1228

MICHIGAN
Medicare Part B
Michigan Blue Cross & Blue Shield
P.O. Box 2201
Detroit, MI 48231-2201

In area code 313: 1-800-482-4045
In area code 517: 1-800-322-0607
In area code 616: 1-800-442-8020
In area code 906: 1-800-562-7802
In Detroit: 313-225-8200

MINNESOTA

Counties of: Anoka, Dakota, Filmore, Goodhue, Hennepin, Houston, Olmstead, Ramsey, Wabasha, Washington, Winona
Medicare/The Travelers Insurance Co.
8120 Penn Avenue
South Bloomington, MN 55431
1-800-352-2762
612-884-7171

Rest of state: Medicare
Blue Shield of Minnesota
P.O. Box 64357
St. Paul, MN 55164
1-800-392-0343
612-456-5070

MISSISSIPPI

Medicare/The Travelers Insurance Co.
P.O. Box 22545
Jackson, MS 39225-2545
1-800-682-5417
601-956-0372

MISSOURI

Counties of: Andrew, Atchison, Bates, Benton, Buchanan, Caldwell, Carroll, Cass, Clay, Clinton, Daviess, DeKalb, Gentry, Grundy, Harrison, Henry, Holt, Jackson, Johnson, Lafayette, Livingston, Mercer, Nodaway, Pettis, Platte, Ray, St. Clair, Saline, Vernon, Worth
Medicare/Blue Shield of Kansas City
P.O. Box 169
Kansas City, MO 64141
1-800-892-5900
816-561-0900

Rest of state: Medicare
General American Life Insurance Co.
P.O. Box 505
St. Louis, MO 63166
1-800-392-3070
314-843-8880

MONTANA
Medicare/Blue Shield of Montana, Inc.
2501 Beltview
P.O. Box 4310
Helena, MT 59604
1-800-332-6146
406-444-8350

NEBRASKA
Medicare Part B
Blue Cross & Blue Shield of Nebraska
P.O. Box 3106
Omaha, NE 68103-0106
1-800-633-1113

NEVADA
Medicare/Aetna Life & Casualty
P.O. Box 37230
Phoenix, AZ 85069
1-800-528-0311

NEW HAMPSHIRE
Medicare
Blue Shield of Massachusetts/Tri-State
P.O. Box 1010
Biddeford, ME 04005
1-800-447-1142

NEW JERSEY
Medicare/Pennsylvania Blue Shield
P.O. Box 400010
Harrisburg, PA 17140-0010
1-800-462-9360

NEW MEXICO
Medicare/Aetna Life & Casualty
P.O. Box 25500
Oklahoma City, OK 73125-0500
1-800-423-2925

In Albuquerque: 505-843-7771

NEW YORK
Counties of: Bronx, Kings, New York, Richmond
Medicare/Empire Blue Cross & Blue Shield
P.O. Box 100
Yorktown Heights, NY 10598
212-490-4444

Counties of: Columbia, Delaware, Dutchess, Greene, Nassau, Orange, Putnam, Rockland, Suffolk, Sullivan, Ulster, Westchester
Medicare/Empire Blue Cross & Blue Shield
P.O. Box 100
Yorktown Heights, NY 10598
1-800-442-8430

County of: Queens
Medicare/Group Health, Inc.
P.O. Box A966, Times Square Station
New York, NY 10036
212-760-6790

Rest of state: Medicare
Blue Shield of Western New York

P.O. Box 5600
Binghamton, NY 13902-0600
607-772-6906
1-800-252-6550

NORTH CAROLINA
Equicor, Inc.
P.O. Box 671
Nashville, TN 37202
1-800-672-3071

NORTH DAKOTA
Medicare/Blue Shield of North Dakota
4510 13th Avenue, S.W.
Fargo, ND 58121-0001
1-800-247-2267
701-282-1100

OHIO
Medicare/Nationwide Mutual Insurance Co.
P.O. Box 57
Columbus, OH 43216
1-800-282-0530
614-249-7157

OKLAHOMA
Medicare/Aetna Life & Casualty
701 N.W. 63rd St., Suite 300
Oklahoma City, OK 73116-7693
1-800-522-9079
405-848-7711

OREGON
Medicare/Aetna Life & Casualty
200 S.W. Market St.

P.O. Box 1997
Portland, OR 97207-1997
1-800-452-0125
503-222-6831

PENNSYLVANIA
Medicare/Pennsylvania Blue Shield
Box 65
Camp Hill, PA 17011
1-800-382-1274

RHODE ISLAND
Medicare/Blue Shield of Rhode Island
444 Westminster Mall
Providence, RI 02901
1-800-662-5170
401-861-2273

SOUTH CAROLINA
Medicare Part B
Blue Cross & Blue Shield of South Carolina
Fontaine Road Business Center
300 Arbor Lake Drive, Suite 1300
Columbia, SC 29223
1-800-922-2340
803-754-0639

SOUTH DAKOTA
Medicare Part B
Blue Shield of North Dakota
4510 13th Avenue, S.W.
Fargo, ND 58121-0001
1-800-437-4762

TENNESSEE
Equicor, Inc.
P.O. Box 1465
Nashville, TN 37202
1-800-342-8900
615-244-5650

TEXAS
Medicare
Blue Cross & Blue Shield of Texas, Inc.
P.O. Box 660031
Dallas, TX 75266-0031
1-800-442-2620

UTAH
Medicare/Blue Shield of Utah
P.O. Box 30269, 2455 Parley's Way
Salt Lake City, UT 84130-0269
1-800-426-3477
801-481-6196

VERMONT
Medicare
Blue Shield of Massachusetts/Tri-State
P.O. Box 1010
Biddeford, ME 04005
1-800-447-1142

VIRGINIA
Counties of: Arlington, Fairfax;
Cities of: Alexandria, Falls Church, Fairfax
Medicare/Pennsylvania Blue Shield
P.O. Box 100
Camp Hill, PA 17011
1-800-233-1124

Rest of state: Medicare/The Travelers Insurance Co.
P.O. Box 26463
Richmond, VA 23261
1-800-552-3423
804-254-4130

WASHINGTON
Medicare/Washington Physicians' Service
Mail to your local Medical Service Bureau.
If you do not know which bureau handles your claim, mail to:
Medicare Washington Physicians' Service
4th and Battery Bldg., 6th Floor
2401 4th Avenue
Seattle, WA 98121

In King County:	1-800-422-4087 206-464-3711
In Spokane:	1-800-572-5256 509-536-4550
In Kitsap:	1-800-552-7114 206-377-5576
In Pierce:	206-597-6530
Others:	Collect if out of call area.

WEST VIRGINIA
Medicare/Nationwide Mutual Insurance Co.
P.O. Box 57
Columbus, OH 43216
1-800-848-0106

WISCONSIN
Medicare/WPS
Box 1787

Madison, WI 53701
1-800-362-7221

In Madison: 608-221-3330
In Milwaukee: 414-931-1071

WYOMING
Equicor, Inc.
P.O. Box 628, 102 Indian Hills Shopping Center
Cheyenne, WY 82003
1-800-442-2371
307-632-9381

AMERICAN SAMOA
Medicare/Hawaii Medical Services Assn.
818 Keeaumoku
Honolulu, HI 96808
808-944-2247

GUAM
Medicare/Aetna Life & Casualty
P.O. Box 3947
Honolulu, HI 96812
808-524-1240

NORTHERN MARIANA ISLANDS
Medicare/Aetna Life & Casualty
P.O. Box 3947
Honolulu, HI 96812
808-524-1240

PUERTO RICO
Medicare/Seguros De Servicio De
Salud De Puerto Rico
Call Box 71391
San Juan, PR 00936

137-800-462-7385
809-759-9191

VIRGIN ISLANDS
Medicare/Seguros De Servicio De
Salud De Puerto Rico
Call Box 71391
San Juan, PR 00936
137-800-462-2970
809-759-9191

State Insurance Regulators

Each state has its own laws and regulations governing all types of insurance. The offices listed in this section are responsible for enforcing these laws, as well as providing the public with information about insurance.

ALABAMA
Alabama Insurance Department
135 S. Union St.
Montgomery, AL 36130-3401
205-269-3550

ALASKA
Alaska Insurance Department
3601 C St., Suite 722
Anchorage, AK 99503
907-562-3626

ARIZONA
Arizona Insurance Department
Consumer Affairs and Investigation Division
3030 N. Third St.
Phoenix, AZ 85012
602-255-4783

ARKANSAS
Arkansas Insurance Department
Consumer Service Division
400 University Tower Bldg.
12th and University Streets
Little Rock, AR 72204
501-371-1813

CALIFORNIA
California Insurance Department
Consumer Services Division
100 Van Ness Ave.
San Francisco, CA 94102
1-800-233-9045
or
600 S. Commonwealth Ave.
Los Angeles, CA 90005
1-800-233-9045

COLORADO
Colorado Insurance Division
303 W. Colfax Ave.
5th Floor
Denver, CO 80204
303-620-4300

CONNECTICUT
Connecticut Insurance Department
165 Capitol Ave.
State Office Building
Room 425
Hartford, CT 06106
203-566-5275

DELAWARE

Delaware Insurance Department
841 Silver Lake Blvd.
Dover, DE 19901
302-736-4251

DISTRICT OF COLUMBIA

District of Columbia Insurance
614 H St., NW
Suite 512
Washington, DC 20001
202-783-3191 727-8009 (202)

FLORIDA

Florida Department of Insurance
State Capitol
Plaza Level Eleven (11)
Tallahassee, FL 32399-0300
904-488-0030

GEORGIA

Georgia Insurance Department
2 Martin L. King, Jr., Drive
7th Floor West Tower
Atlanta, GA 30334
404-656-2056

HAWAII

Hawaii Department of Commerce and Consumer Affairs
Insurance Division
P.O. Box 3614
Honolulu, HI 96811
808-548-5450

IDAHO
Idaho Insurance Department
Public Service Department
500 S. 10th St.
Boise, ID 83720
208-334-2250

ILLINOIS
Illinois Insurance Department
320 W. Washington St.
4th Floor
Springfield, IL 62767
217-782-4515

INDIANA
Indiana Insurance Department
311 W. Washington St.
Suite 300
Indianapolis, IN 46204
317-232-2395

IOWA
Iowa Insurance Division
Lucas State Office Bldg.
E. 12th and Walnut Streets
6th Floor
Des Moines, IA 50319
515-281-5705

KANSAS
Kansas Insurance Department
420 S.W. 9th St.
Topeka, KS 66612
913-296-3071

KENTUCKY
Kentucky Insurance Department
229 W. Main St.
P.O. Box 517
Frankfort, KY 40602
502-564-3630

LOUISIANA
Louisiana Insurance Department
P.O. Box 94214
Baton Rouge, LA 70804-9214
504-342-5900

MAINE
Maine Bureau of Insurance
Consumer Division
State House, Station 34
Augusta, ME 04333
207-582-8707

MARYLAND
Maryland Insurance Department 1-800-492-6116
Complaints and Investigation Unit
501 St. Paul Place
Baltimore, MD 21202-2272
301-333-2792

MASSACHUSETTS
Massachusetts Insurance Division
Consumer Services Section
280 Friend St.
Boston, MA 02114
617-727-3357

MICHIGAN
Michigan Insurance Department
P.O. Box 30220
Lansing, MI 48909
517-373-0220

MINNESOTA
Minnesota Insurance Department
Department of Commerce
500 Metro Square Bldg.
7th and Roberts Streets
St. Paul, MN 55101
612-296-4026

MISSISSIPPI
Mississippi Insurance Department
Consumer Assistance Division
P.O. Box 79
Jackson, MS 39205
601-359-3569

MISSOURI
Missouri Division of Insurance
Consumer Services Section
P.O. Box 690
Jefferson City, MO 65102-0690
314-751-2640

MONTANA
Montana Insurance Department
126 North Sanders
Mitchell Building
P.O. Box 4009, Room 270
Helena, MT 59604
406-444-2040

NEBRASKA
Nebraska Insurance Department
Terminal Building
941 O St., Suite 400
Lincoln, NE 68508
402-471-2201

NEVADA
Nevada Department of Commerce
Insurance Division
201 S. Fall St.
Room 316
Carson City, NV 89701
702-885-4270

NEW HAMPSHIRE
New Hampshire Insurance Department
Life and Health Division
169 Manchester St.
Concord, NH 03301
603-271-2261

NEW JERSEY
New Jersey Insurance Department
20 W. State St.
Roebling Building
Trenton, NJ 08625
609-292-4757

NEW MEXICO
New Mexico Insurance Department
P.O. Box 1269
Santa Fe, NM 87504-1269
505-827-4500

NEW YORK
New York Insurance Department
160 W. Broadway
New York, NY 10013

New York City: 212-602-0203

Toll-free (within state outside of NYC):
1-800-342-3736

NORTH CAROLINA
North Carolina Insurance Department
Consumer Insurance Information
Dobbs Building
P.O. Box 26387
Raleigh, NC 27611
919-733-2004

NORTH DAKOTA
North Dakota Insurance Department
Capitol Building
5th Floor
Bismarck, ND 58505
701-224-2440

OHIO
Ohio Insurance Department
Consumer Services Division
2100 Stella Court
Columbus, OH 43215
614-644-2673

OKLAHOMA
Oklahoma Insurance Department
P.O. Box 53408
Oklahoma City, OK 73152-3408
405-521-2828

OREGON

Oregon Department of Insurance and Finance
Insurance Division/Consumer Advocate
21 Labor and Industry Bldg.
Salem, OR 97310
503-378-4484

PENNSYLVANIA

Pennsylvania Insurance Department
1326 Strawberry Square
Harrisburg, PA 17120
717-787-3289

RHODE ISLAND

Rhode Island Insurance Division
233 Richmond St.
Suite 233
Providence, RI 02903-4233
401-277-2223

SOUTH CAROLINA

South Carolina Insurance Department
Consumer Assistance Section
P.O. Box 100105
Columbia, SC 29202-3105
803-737-6140

SOUTH DAKOTA

South Dakota Insurance Department
Enforcement
500 E. Capitol
Pierre, SD 57501
605-773-3563

TENNESSEE
Tennessee Insurance Department
Department of Commerce and Insurance
Policyholders Service Section
1880 West End Ave.
14th Floor
Nashville, TN 37219-5318
1-800-342-4031

TEXAS
Texas Board of Insurance
Complaints Division
1110 San Jacinto Blvd.
Austin, TX 78701-1998
512-463-6501

UTAH
Utah Insurance Department
Consumer Services
P.O. Box 45803
Salt Lake City, UT 84145
801-530-6400

VERMONT
Vermont Department of Banking and Insurance
Consumer Complaint Division
120 State St.
Montpelier, VT 05602
802-828-3301

VIRGINIA
Virginia Insurance Department
Consumer Services Division
700 Jefferson Bldg.
P.O. Box 1157

Richmond, VA 23209
804-786-7691

WASHINGTON
Washington Insurance Department
Insurance Building AQ21
Olympia, WA 98504
206-753-7300

WEST VIRGINIA
West Virginia Insurance Department
2019 Washington St., E
Charleston, WV 25305
304-348-3386

WISCONSIN
Wisconsin Insurance Department
Complaints Department
P.O. Box 7873
Madison, WI 53707
608-266-0103

WYOMING
Wyoming Insurance Department
Herschler Building
122 W. 25th St.
Cheyenne, WY 82002
307-777-7401

AMERICAN SAMOA
American Samoa Insurance Department
Office of the Governor
Pago Pago, AS 96797
011-684-633-4116

GUAM
Guam Insurance Department
P.O. Box 2796
Agana, GU 96910
or
855 W. Marine Drive
011-671-477-1040
(22 hrs. earlier than CST)

PUERTO RICO
Puerto Rico Insurance Department
Fernandez Juncos Station
P.O. Box 8330
Santurce, PR 00910
809-722-8686

VIRGIN ISLANDS
Virgin Islands Insurance Department
Kongens Garde No. 18
St. Thomas, VI 00802
809-774-2991

State Agencies on Aging

The offices listed are responsible for coordinating services for older Americans.

ALABAMA
Alabama Commission on Aging
136 Catoma St.
Montgomery, AL 36130
205-261-5743
Toll free (within state):
1-800-243-5463

ALASKA
Older Alaskans Commission
P.O. Box C, MS 0209
Juneau, AK 99811
907-465-3250

ARIZONA
Department of Economic Security
Aging and Adult Administration
1400 W. Washington St.
Phoenix, AZ 85007
602-254-4446

ARKANSAS
Division of Aging and Adult Services
Donaghey Plaza South
Suite 1417
7th and Main Streets
P.O. Box 1437/Slot 1412
Little Rock, AR 72203-1437
501-682-2441

CALIFORNIA
Department of Aging
1600 K St.
Sacramento, CA 95814
916-322-3887

COLORADO
Aging and Adult Services
Department of Social Services
1575 Sherman St., 10th Floor
Denver, CO 80203-1714
303-866-5905

CONNECTICUT
Department on Aging
175 Main St.
Hartford, CT 06106
203-566-7772

Toll free (within state):
1-800-443-9946

DELAWARE
Division of Aging
Department of Health and Social Services

1901 N. Dupont Highway
New Castle, DE 19720
302-421-6791

DISTRICT OF COLUMBIA
Office on Aging
Executive Office of the Mayor
1424 K St., NW
2nd Floor
Washington, DC 20005
202-724-5626
202-724-5622

FLORIDA
Florida Department of Insurance
The Capitol
Tallahassee, FL 32301

Toll free (within state):
1-800-342-2762

GEORGIA
Office of Aging
Department of Human Resources
878 Peachtree St., NE
Room 632
Atlanta, GA 30309
404-894-5333

HAWAII
Executive Office on Aging
335 Merchant St.
Room 241
Honolulu, HI 96813
808-548-2593

IDAHO
Office on Aging
Statehouse, Room 114
Boise, ID 83720
208-334-3833

ILLINOIS
Department on Aging
421 E. Capitol Ave.
Springfield, IL 62701
217-785-2870

INDIANA
Department of Human Services
251 North Illinois
P.O. Box 7083
Indianapolis, IN 46207-7083
317-232-1139

IOWA
Department of Elder Affairs
Suite 236, Jewett Building
914 Grand Ave.
Des Moines, IA 50319
515-281-5187

KANSAS
Department on Aging
122-S, Docking State Office Bldg.
915 SW Harrison
Topeka, KS 66612-1500
913-296-4986

KENTUCKY
Division for Aging Services
Department for Social Services
275 E. Main St.
Frankfort, KY 40621
502-564-6930

LOUISIANA
Governor's Office of Elderly Affairs
P.O. Box 80374
Baton Rouge, LA 70898-0374
504-925-1700

MAINE
Maine Committee of Aging
State House, Station 127
Augusta, ME 04333
207-289-3658

MARYLAND
State Agency on Aging
301 W. Preston St.
Baltimore, MD 21201
301-225-1102

MASSACHUSETTS
Executive Office of Elder Affairs
38 Chauncy St.
Boston, MA 02111
617-727-7750

Toll free (within state):
1-800-882-2003

MICHIGAN
Office of Services to the Aging
P.O. Box 30026
Lansing, MI 48909
517-373-8230

MINNESOTA
Minnesota Board on Aging
Metro Square Building
Suite 204
121 E. Seventh St.
St. Paul, MN 55101
612-296-2770

MISSISSIPPI
Council on Aging
301 W. Pearl St.
Jackson, MS 39203-3092
601-949-2070

Toll free (within state):
1-800-222-7622

MISSOURI
Missouri Division of Insurance
Truman Building 630
P.O. Box 690
Jefferson City, MO 65102-0690

Toll free (within state):
1-800-235-5503

MONTANA
Department of Family Services
P.O. Box 8005

Helena, MT 59604
406-444-5900

NEBRASKA
Department on Aging
Legal Services Developer
State Office Building
301 Centennial Mall South
Lincoln, NE 68509
402-471-2306

NEVADA
Department of Human Resources
Division for Aging Services
505 E. King St.
Room 101
Carson City, NV 89710
702-885-4210

NEW HAMPSHIRE
Department of Health and Human Services
Division of Elderly and Adult Services
6 Hazen Drive
Concord, NH 03301
603-271-4390

NEW JERSEY
Department of Community Affairs
Division on Aging
South Broad and Front Sts.
CN 807
Trenton, NJ 08625-0807
609-292-0920

NEW MEXICO
Agency on Aging
La Villa Rivera Building
4th Floor
224 E. Palace Ave.
Santa Fe, NM 87501
505-827-7640

Toll free (within state):
1-800-432-2080

NEW YORK
State Office for the Aging
Agency Building
#2 Empire State Plaza
Albany, NY 12223-0001
518-474-5731

Toll free (within state):
1-800-342-9871

NORTH CAROLINA
Department of Human Resources
Division of Aging
1985 Umstead Drive
Raleigh, NC 27603
919-733-3983

NORTH DAKOTA
Department of Human Services
Aging Services Division
State Capitol Building
Bismarck, ND 58505
701-224-2577

OHIO
Department of Aging
50 W. Broad St.
9th Floor
Columbus, OH 43266-0501
614-466-1220

OKLAHOMA
Department of Human Services
Aging Services Division
P.O. Box 25352
Oklahoma City, OK 73125
405-521-2327

OREGON
Department of Human Resources
Senior Services Division
313 Public Service Bldg.
Salem, OR 97310
503-378-4636

Toll free (within state):
1-800-232-3020

PENNSYLVANIA
Department of Aging
231 State St.
Barto Building
Harrisburg, PA 17101
717-783-1550

RHODE ISLAND
Department of Elderly Affairs
79 Washington St.
Providence, RI 02903
401-277-2858

SOUTH CAROLINA
Commission on Aging
400 Arbor Lake Drive
Suite B-500
Columbia, SC 29223
803-735-0210

SOUTH DAKOTA
Agency on Aging
Adult Services and Aging
Richard F. Kneip Building
700 Governors Drive
Pierre, SD 57501-2291
605-773-3656

TENNESSEE
Commission on Aging
Commerce and Insurance Department
Volunteer Plaza
James Robinson Parkway
Nashville, TN 37219-5573
615-741-2241

TEXAS
Department on Aging
P.O. Box 12786
Capitol Station
Austin, TX 78711
512-444-2727

UTAH
Division of Aging & Adult Services
120 North 200 West
P.O. Box 45500

Salt Lake City, UT 84145-0500
801-538-3910

VERMONT
Office on Aging
Waterbury Complex
103 S. Main St.
Waterbury, VT 05676
802-241-2400

VIRGINIA
Department for the Aging
18th Floor
101 N. 14th St.
Richmond, VA 23219
804-225-2271

Toll free (within state):
1-800-552-4464

WASHINGTON
Aging & Adult Services Administration
Department of Social & Health Services
Mail Stop OB-44-A
Olympia, WA 98504
206-586-3768

WEST VIRGINIA
Commission on Aging
State Capitol Complex
Holly Grove
Charleston, WV 25305
304-348-3317

Toll free (within state):
1-800-642-3671

WISCONSIN
Bureau on Aging
Department of Health and Social Services
P.O. Box 7851
Madison, WI 53707
608-266-2536

Toll free (within state):
1-800-242-1060

WYOMING
Commission on Aging
Hathaway Building
1st Floor
Cheyenne, WY 82002
307-777-7986

Toll free (within state):
1-800-442-2766

AMERICAN SAMOA
Territorial Administration on Aging
Government of American Samoa
Pago Pago, AS 96799
684-633-1251

FEDERATED STATES OF MICRONESIA
State Agency on Aging
Office of Health Services
Federated States of Micronesia
Ponape, E.C.I. 96941

GUAM
Division of Senior Citizens
Department of Public Health and Social Services
P.O. Box 2816

Agana, GU 96910
671-734-2942

NORTHERN MARIANA ISLANDS
Department of Community and Cultural Affairs
Civic Center
Commonwealth of the Northern Mariana Islands
Saipan, CM 96950
670-234-6011

PALAU
State Agency on Aging
Department of Social Services
Republic of Palau
Koror, Palau 96940

PUERTO RICO
Governors Office of Elderly Affairs
Gericulture Commission
Box 11398
Santurce, PR 00910
809-722-2429 or 722-0225

REPUBLIC OF THE MARSHALL ISLANDS
State Agency on Aging
Department of Social Services
Republic of the Marshall Islands
Marjuro, Marshall Islands 96960

VIRGIN ISLANDS
Department of Human Services
Barbel Plaza South
Charlotte Amalie
St. Thomas, VI 00802
809-774-0930

Glossary of Medicare-Related Terms

actual charge the amount a physician or supplier actually bills a patient for a particular medical service or supply. (This may differ from the customary, prevailing, and/or reasonable charges under Medicare.)

assignment a process through which a doctor or supplier agrees to accept the Medicare program's payment as payment in full except for specific coinsurance and deductible amounts required of the patient.

carrier a private insurance organization that contracts with the federal government to handle claims from doctors and suppliers of services covered by Medicare medical insurance.

claim a request to a carrier or intermediary by a beneficiary or a provider acting on behalf of a beneficiary for payment of benefits under Medicare.

coinsurance a cost-sharing requirement which provides that a beneficiary will assume a portion or percentage of the costs of covered services.

competitive medical plan (CMP) a prepayment health care plan. CMPs with medicare contracts offer Medicare beneficiaries all services covered by fee-for-service Medicare.

customary charge the amount that a doctor or supplier most frequently charges for each separate service and supply furnished.

deductible the amount of expense a beneficiary must first incur before Medicare begins payment for covered services.

health maintenance organization (HMO) a prepayment health care plan. HMOs with Medicare contracts offer Medicare beneficiaries all services covered by fee-for-service Medicare.

home health agency a public or private organization that specializes in giving skilled nursing services and other therapeutic services such as physical therapy in a beneficiary's home.

hospice a program operated by a public agency or private organization which engages primarily in providing pain relief, symptom management, and supportive services for terminally ill people and their families.

hospital insurance the part of Medicare that helps pay for inpatient hospital care, some inpatient care in a skilled nursing facility, home health care, and hospice care.

intermediary a private insurance organization that contracts with the federal government to handle Medicare payment for services by hospitals, skilled nursing facilities, and home health agencies paid through the hospital insurance program.

medical insurance the part of Medicare that helps pay for medically necessary doctors' services, outpatient hospital services, and a number of other medical services and supplies that are not covered by the hospital insurance part of Medicare as well as some home health services.

Medigap policy private health insurance designed to supplement Medicare.

outpatient facility a facility designed to provide health and medical services to individuals who have not checked into the hospital.

participating physician or supplier a physician or supplier who agrees to accept assignment on all Medicare claims.

peer review organizations (PROs) groups of practicing doctors and other health care professionals under contract to the federal government to review the care provided to Medicare patients.

prepayment health plans health care providers such as health maintenance organizations (HMOs) and competitive medical plans (CMPs).

prevailing charge based on the customary charges for covered medical insurance services or items, the prevailing charge is the maximum charge Medicare can approve for any item or service.

prospective payment system (PPS) a process started in 1983 under which hospitals are paid fixed amounts based on the principal diagnosis for each Medicare hospital stay.

quality review organizations (QROs) groups of practicing doctors and other health care professionals under contract to the federal government to review the care provided to Medicare patients.

reasonable charges amounts approved by the Medicare carrier which will be either the customary charge, the prevailing charge, or the actual charge, whichever is the lowest.

skilled nursing facility a specially qualified facility which has the staff and equipment to provide skilled nursing care or rehabilitation services and other related health services.

supplemental health insurance also called Medigap insurance—private health insurance designed to fill some of the gaps in Medicare.

Index

Improve Your Health with These Important Books

(To order, please use order form on the next page)

Good Cholesterol, Bad Cholesterol by Eli M. Roth, M.D., and Sandra Streicher, R.N. $8.95
Praised by experts as the finest book on cholesterol, this book covers every aspect of the cholesterol equation in a clearly understandable style. "A valuable guide into the benefits of a disease-preventive lifestyle." William C. DeVries, M.D.

Controlling High Blood Pressure, edited by Frans H.H. Leenen, M.D., and R. Brian Haynes, M.D. $15.95
In this book, ten of North America's top hypertension specialists, each writing a chapter, cover every aspect of dealing with hypertension. Highly informative, comprehensive, and easy to understand.

Immune for Life by Arnold Fox, M.D., and Barry Fox, Ph.D. . . . $9.95
In the final analysis, most diseases are caused by a failure of the immune system to respond correctly. In *Immune for Life*, Dr. Fox shows the reader how to adopt a lifestyle that promotes a strong immune system, which he calls "our doctor within." Included is a program encompassing nutrition, mental attitude, and physical exercise.

Retin-A and Other Youth Miracles by Joseph P. Bark, M.D., with a foreword by Albert Kligman, M.D., Ph.D. $9.95
This is the first book by a dermatologist on the subject of Retin-A. It addresses, in depth, the virtues as well as the side effects of this important medicine. In addition, it covers other "youth miracles" including the elimination of unsightly veins in the legs, reversing hair loss, and rearranging or eliminating fat tissue.

Health-Related Cookbooks

Lean and Luscious, and *More Lean and Luscious* by Bobbie Hinman and Millie Snyder . . . . each book $14.95
These two cookbooks each offer over 400 recipes. Each recipe is designed for today's low-fat, low-cholesterol, high-fiber lifestyle. Each recipe comes with an at-a-glance nutritional breakdown. Spiral comb-bound for easy reading.

Oat Cuisine by Bobbie Hinman $12.95
Over 200 delicious recipes to help you lower your cholesterol level. With a foreword by Peter O. Kwiterovich, Jr.

Dairy-Free Cookbook by Jane Zukin $18.95
For people with little or no milk tolerance, this is a life saver. Included are recipes for both adults and children and guidelines for eating out. Recommended for gastroenterologists, internists, and all who suffer from milk allergy or lactose deficiency.

FILL IN AND MAIL . . . TODAY

PRIMA PUBLISHING
P.O. BOX 1260MED
ROCKLIN, CA 95677

USE YOUR VISA/MC AND ORDER BY PHONE:
(916) 624-5718 (M–F 9–4 PST)

Dear People at Prima,
I'd like to order the following titles:

Quantity	**Title**	**Amount**
______	________________________	______
______	________________________	______
______	________________________	______
______	________________________	______
______	________________________	______

Subtotal	$	______
Postage & Handling*	$	3.00
Sales Tax	$	______
TOTAL (U.S. funds only)	$	______

*Include $3.00 postage and handling for the first book ordered, and an additional $1.00 per title for multiple book orders.

☐ Check enclosed for $ ______ (payable to Prima Publishing)

Charge my ☐ Mastercard ☐ Visa

Account No. ____________________ Exp. Date ____________

Signature ________________________________

Your Name ________________________________

Address ________________________________

City/State/Zip ________________________________

Daytime Telephone ________________________________

YOU MUST BE SATISFIED, OR YOUR MONEY BACK!!!
Thank You for Your Order